Recount

Recount

Cliff Prothero

G.W. & A. Hesketh, Ormskirk & Northridge

First published 1982 by G.W. & A. Hesketh, P.O. Box 8, Aughton Street, Ormskirk, Lancashire L39 5HH, Great Britain, and of 18765 Tuba Street, Northridge, California 91324, U.S.A.

Design by G.W. & A. Hesketh, P.O. Box 8, Ormskirk, L39 5HH.
Printed and bound in Great Britain by Sturdy Print and Design Unit, Westgate, 61-63 Sandy Lane Centre, Skelmersdale, Lancashire.
Typesetting and origination by Lloyd Williams, 22 Union Street, Southport.

ISBN O 905777 33 6 Paperback.

Manuscript received March 1981.

For my wife Vi who sacrificed much to enable me to serve the Labour Party.

Contents

List of Illustrations

Foreword

This record has been typed at odd moments over several years, by me using two fingers on an old typewriter which I bought secondhand back in 1940.

As I continue my journey through Memory Lane I am reminded that I joined a trade union almost seventy years ago and my membership of the Labour Party goes back over sixty years. Both movements have a very warm place in my heart because the main purpose is to be of service to ordinary folk.

In politics, Socialism to me is a way of life as we strive for brotherhood and friendship knowing that people and their welfare are more important than constitutions.

It is now February 1981 and I acknowledge that I am living on borrowed time and in writing my memoirs I am not seeking any credit or financial gain. My purpose is simply to place on record in all humility certain events in particular those of my own personal experience in the hope that some future historian will at least find a thread of something worthwhile in what I have written.

Some of my friends who know of my struggles and sacrifices of the past have asked me "Are you bitter because of what happened to you personally during the 1926 Strike and the years of depression that followed?" My answer is definitely no, because I have kept my faith in Him who came and declared, "I came that men may have life and may have it in all its fullness". This faith has always been very precious to me whether I am beside still waters or climbing rugged mountains. I have on a number of occasions drawn much comfort from the following lines, whose author is, sadly, unknown to me:

> For every hill I've had to climb,
> For every stone that bruised my feet,
> For all the tears and sweat and grime,
> For the blinding storms and burning heat,
> My heart still sings a grateful song,
> These were the things that made me strong.

Cliff Prothero
Penarth, February 1981

Acknowledgements

I should like to thank Dr. Rev. D. Ben Rees and Peter Stead for their great services in helping me, Betty Thomas, Freda Coles and Jeannette Kennedy for their loyal service to me as key members of my staff, and Margaret Bosley for the encouragement given me to publish.

Cliff Prothero

1

Early Years

I was born on September 23rd 1898 at number 129 Robert Street, Ynysybwl, a working class home. It appears that I made my entry into this world just at the end of a six months' strike in the South Wales Coal Mining Industry. In later years my Mother informed me that I arrived when things were not too good financially and she found it difficult to find the money to travel to Pontypridd to register my birth.

Both my parents were Welsh and spoke and understood the Welsh Language. My Mother came from Pontlottyn at the top end of the Rhymney Valley in the county of Glamorgan and my Father came from Near Knighton in the county of Radnorshire.

I received an elementary education at the Tre-Robert Boys' School, Ynysybwl there was no co-education in those days. As a small lad I would spend some time on Saturday evenings on or near what was known as the village square where there would be two or three speakers advocating a change in the system to one of Socialism. This subject was of course very unpopular at that time and as the speakers like Johnny Morgan and his brother Abel along with on occasions Will May, were spending much energy in propounding the advantages of Socialism and the need for a new social order, they naturally had no sympathy for the Capitalist System and spent much time and words in its condemnation. There were occasions when those who listened were less in number than the speakers but this did not deter them in what was to them a mission. It must be remembered that I am writing about a time when there were very few Socialists in the village and those who were in sympathy with this new doctrine were considered to be very queer people. However I would listen and try hard to understand what the speakers were talking about and indeed what was the need to change the system. I, of course, was too young to understand but there was some attraction in listening to speakers who were in their way sincere in their belief but with no visible supporters.

Looking back over the years to those meetings on that village square which did not appear to serve any useful purpose when they were held, on reflection I ask myself, "Did all that was said at those meetings fall on stony ground, or was the seed sown on behalf of Socialism which came to fruition in later years?"

Ynysybwl was a compact village with a population of almost five thousand living very much as a community of its own. It is about three and a half miles north of Pontypridd in the Vale of the Clydach with mountains to the east, and to the west with the mountain of Llanwonno to the north. So the village itself stands nestled at the foot of Llanwonno. It was serviced by a railway from Pontypridd with a small train which of course could go on further than Ynysybwl. This train would be well patronized and particularly on Saturdays when so many people would take an afternoon out for shopping or for an evening's entertainment. Pontypridd was a very busy town with its many large shops and its two markets the one under cover and the other outside quite near the main shopping centre. This town was a centre of activity and this was probably because of its very favourable position for it was in fact the gateway to industrial districts of Rhondda, Aberdare and Merthyr. Standing on Pontypridd Railway Station late on any Saturday evening, a voice could be heard calling out "Any more for the Bwl, hurry up for the Bwl". A stranger would be a little puzzled wondering what was meant by what he could hear. It would simply be the voice of a Railway Employee informing passengers that the last train was about to leave for Ynysybwl on that day.

At school I was doing reasonably well and my teacher was anxious for me to sit a scholarship examination with a view of going forward for higher education, which if successful would mean me going to the Grammar School at Pontypridd. I was quite interested and then very suddenly I decided that I would not sit the examination. My teacher went and approached my parents and asked them to persuade me to change my mind because in his view I stood a very good chance of success. However I had made up my mind and nothing would cause me to go back on the decision which I had taken.

The Head Master and the teachers at the school were grand people, they all lived in the village and took a keen interest not only in the children but also in the public affairs of the community. They were always available to give advice to parents and children alike and were very popular with all sections of the population.

In the realms of sport there were two teams in Ynysybwl, the one played soccer and the other played rugby, the latter was named the Village Boys. The school was represented by its teachers playing in each of the teams so a number of boys from the school would be seen and heard supporting those of our teachers at a soccer match, also the others at a rugby match. I, at a very early age, became very fond of sport and almost idolised the players and in particular our playing teachers.

From Ynysybwl there were two forms of transport the one was by train and the other was on foot. I can well remember one occasion which was little out of the ordinary when there was an important match at Taff Vale Park Treforest which was situated about one and a half miles below Pontypridd. The contending teams were the Wallabies (the Australians) and Glamorgan.

This was, if I remember correctly, in the year 1908, so I was at that time quite a small boy but with a few friends from the School made our way which meant a total walk of about 10 miles to see a great game of rugby. It was worth the effort because we enjoyed ourselves very much and particularly when one of the players kicked the ball high and hard away out of the playing field and it dropped into the river Taff and was carried away in the direction of Cardiff.

At the age of 13 years I left school and decided to go to work which meant in coal mining because it was the only industry in the village, there were in fact

2

three collieries, the one big one was the Lady Windsor Pit where my father and brother worked. This pit is still at the time of writing producing coal. Then there was a small drift, which means a hole driven down into the mountain at a gradient, and at the other end of Ynysybwl, on the side of the road as you go towards Pontypridd there was a small level known as Darran-Du. A colliery of that kind was called a level though it is driven into the hill with a very slight gradient to allow water to run out to the surface. I favoured this colliery maybe because I would be able if necessary to walk in or out whereas if I went to work in the pit I would be taken down and brought back up in a cage. My first job was with three brothers and it was understood that I would be available to help anyone of them.

I worked for eight hours per day and for six days per week and it was very hard work and at the end of the day I would be glad to get back home. My wages were two shillings per day and on receiving my first pay I was given an extra six pence pocket money because my bosses said I had worked so hard.

We were taken into this little coal mine in horse drawn trams every morning and brought out by the same method at the end of the day. In the particular part where I was working it was known that we were heading toward old workings from where coal had been mined a long time ago and there was a possibility of a lot of water being ahead of us but no one could be sure. However one day I was told to go and work with a man in another part and this I did without question because I knew that those in charge were thinking of my safety. At the end of the shift I was making my way from the coal face to a place known as the 'Double Parting', a dual carriageway where the empty trams were brought in and the full ones taken out. This would also be the point where we would get into the trams and be taken out to the surface. Before getting to this place I was met by some men coming toward me and were waving their lamps and telling all within hearing distance to go back to a higher point of the mine because water had been struck and the mine was flooded. Needless to say I with others hastened to that higher part where we would be safe from the on-rushing water.

We were quite a little company and after resting for a while feeling quite safe from the water because this coal mine with a slight gradient going down toward the surface would enable the water to run out and could not very well reach the point where we were unless there was some blockage. As we were feeling quite safe there was another scare because our oil lamps which we normally wore in our caps were not burning so brightly as usual and were in fact giving less light and this was noticed by one of the men who saw the danger and said in a very firm voice, "Come along we cannot stay here any longer because where our lamps will not keep alight we will not keep alive under such conditions". In going to the upper part of the mine to be safe from the water we were in fact confronted with another danger that was the foul air coming with the water from the old workings and different to the water this foul air would find its way to the higher parts of the colliery. Then again the upper workings which were the farthest parts from the surface could be the most dangerous for the lack of fresh air. The man who called upon us to leave that spot and face the water was of course an experienced miner and it is such an advantage to have such a man near at hand when there is any danger about. So no one questioned the advice but we all made our way back to take our chance against water which would give us a better chance than remaining to inhale foul air.

We arrived at the 'Double Parting' or quite near when we were met by a Colliery Official who advised us to proceed carefully in our walk toward the surface: there would be no horse drawn trams on that day, the horses having made their way to the surface and again there was the danger of the rushing water carrying with it large pieces of timber and even large doors which are constructed and placed in position to conduct the flow of air and as these would be closed against the flow of water they would be dislodged and carried away by force. The Colliery Official gave an order that "no boy was to walk on his own so if there is one near to you take him by the hand". A man whom I hardly knew took hold of my hand and said "come along and don't let go of my hand". The water was rushing past us from behind and it was up to my shoulders because I was just a small boy and after walking for a while with my heart in my mouth and my feet feeling very heavy I continued to press on with the man holding on to me and giving me words of comfort. Walking out from that colliery was just like walking in a dark tunnel and eventually a small spot of day-light could be seen a long way off and as we plodded forward the spot was getting larger as we were nearing the surface. I was glad to get out safely and my thoughts turned to my family, friends and home where there there would be a welcome awaiting me. Not that my thoughts had been very far away from family and friends for the past few hours!

The news had already spread through the village and neighbours would be at home to give help and support in every way. There were no pit head baths in those days and very few houses had a proper bath so like most other people I lived in an ordinary house where on arriving home from work any day I would bath in a tub placed in front of a coal fire. On this day as soon as I arrived home, my wet dirty clothes were taken off me and I was directed to a tub of water in its usual place. The water had been in all probability boiled in more than one house and poured into the tub in readiness for me. As I stepped into the tub of hot water a neighbour emptied a tin of mustard into the water and said "that will prevent you catching a cold". This was just an example of the friendliness of neighbours that was at that time to be found in any coal mining village in South Wales. These people were the salt of the earth and in some ways it might have been as a result of living in such a compact community.

After some days I went back to work in Darran-Du and to the very spot where the water had broken through and it was very revealing to see how the pressure of water had pushed back one seam of coal. The system employed for the ventilation of the mine had by now been properly restored because it had no doubt been damaged by the rushing water breaking down doors. So now the foul air which had come from the old workings had been cleared away and replaced by fresh air.

Those were very impressionable years of which I have a vivid recollection not of the colliery only but of what was happening in other directions also. My parents were religious people and members of Zion English Baptist Church which meant that I had to go to services three times on Sunday and at least one or two evenings during the week attending the Band of Hope and Christian Endeavour or some other event. There were leaders in that Chapel who made a tremendous impression on me and I can still call to mind two men in particular who were very active in all the affairs of Zion but were also leaders in the political and cultural life of the village and indeed of the district. They were William Watkins and Richard Woosnam to whom I looked up and respected for they were men who had convictions by which they stood and battled away against much opposition in their endeavour to get fair play for the ordinary people. I still believe that I owe a lot to those two men and their colleagues who worked along with them at Zion Baptist Chapel. The building where we worshipped was called the chapel and not the church as far as non-conformists were concerned. The chapel would be full on Sundays and there would be a fair number present at the services held during the week. There would of course be Special Services such as Sunday School Anniversary for which I would have to rehearse for weeks in order to recite something appropriate. I had a good memory but in my own interest I invariably thought that the shortest poem was the most suitable to recite but my parents had other views so it meant that I would have to work very hard in order to be equal to the task. I am sure that I gave some trouble to the leaders of the Band of Hope and other organisations which I was able to attend. However having been brought up in a religious home it is not difficult for me to appreciate and understand the need for a code by which to live, of regulations to be observed. For instance there should be no needle and cotton used in our house on a Sunday, neither should there be any washing of clothes, and so on, in fact there should be no work done on a Sunday which could be done on some other day. My parents felt very strongly that Sunday was set apart for worship and rest from labour and in this way the week would commence in such a way as to give strength and courage for the days ahead. After coming home from Sunday evening service we would as a family sit around a coal fire and sing some of our favourite hymns from the Sankey hymn book. This continued for years and when I became a young man we still had our hymn singing sessions and would also then discuss the sermon which we had heard in the service. This was very good training for membership of future discussion groups. It would help each member of the family to get to know that as we shared our views, it helped us to understand each other much better. That was a time when preaching was very important and particularly to non-conformists who attached so much importance to the preaching of the Word and at that time there was no such thing as a microphone so the congregation had to hear every word and it was the preacher's responsibility to make sure that his voice was clear and carried to all parts of the chapel. This is an art which is on the way out but when I was a boy it was considered that the pulpit was not a suitable place to give a lecture or a homely chat. A sermon was not some talk given on a Sunday evening and then forgotten about, it was talked about by groups of people during the week and attempts made to put it into practice not by church members only but by others who got to know of the sermon. The church building was the centre of much activity where friendship could be formed and cultivated and where conversation would always be helpful. Furthermore there was nowhere else to go in the village so we went to the chapel where we also had much fun which we made ourselves and maybe this is what is lacking today. I have no regret that I had to attend chapel so often because it gave me a firm foundation and an outlook on life which I have been able to link up with the kind of Socialism which I have attempted to follow and accept as a way of life. It gave me to understand that we are so dependent upon other people and that "Man is not an island unto himself" but is a member of a community and must be concerned with other people and the conditions under which they live.

The influence of the Sunday School and Church has remained with me for which I am most grateful and hope it will continue for all time. Some of the hymns we sang at services on Sunday at the Chapel and indeed at our singing sessions at home have remained with me and one in particular which I liked and still like is the one which in itself is a challenge and here is the chorus:

> Dare to be a Daniel
> Dare to stand alone,
> Dare to have a purpose firm
> And dare to make it known.

I mentioned that this was a challenge it is also a guiding line which if followed through life may create difficulties for oneself yet on the other hand would give confidence and assurance when in doubt. In addition to that little chorus I have had for many years a little plaque with the words of Confucius "To know what is right and fear to do it is cowardice" hanging on the wall in my living room as a reminder to do that which I consider to be right and put up with what may follow.

Military Service

When I was almost fourteen years of age my family moved to Glynneath another coal mining village in the beautiful Vale of Neath and although in new surroundings the people were very friendly and helpful. My father, my brother, and I went to work in Aberpergwm Colliery which is still a going concern. I soon took an interest in Trade Union affairs and at the age of fifteen spoke for the first time in a meeting of Aberpergwm Lodge. I was as expected shouted down and reminded of my age but I persisted and the shouting against me became louder and louder with some unpleasant threats. Then a man by the name of John Howells whom I remember to this day stood up and said to the Chairman and to the meeting, "This boy is a member of our organisation and I have no idea what he wishes to say and I may disagree with every word he speaks but in the name of fair play I demand that he be afforded the right to speak". This rather took the meeting by surprise and the chairman decided that I be allowed to speak. I have often wondered what might have happened to me if I had not been given the right to speak as a paying member of the South Wales Miners' Federation and to participate fully in the general meeting. I will never forget John Howells who stood by me and in all probability I owe much to him for my activities in the Trade Union Movement from that day forward. The Colliery was situated on a large estate owned by Mr. Godfrey Williams who lived in Aberpergwm House. He was not an absentee landlord but was very much concerned with what was happening in the Colliery and on the estate.

On certain days every effort would be made to produce more coal than had been produced on any other day. We called these "record breaking days" and Mr. Godfrey Williams would be found on such days on the Colliery surface pushing trams of coal so that they could be weighed quickly and then tipped down on to the screen. Yes, he would work for the whole day giving a helping hand wherever it was required.

The Coal Owner also owned a large number of houses occupied by his employees, a butcher shop, a grocery stores and also supplied the houses with electricity. The houses were all situated near to the colliery in one compact estate with the shopping facilities at hand. This meant that the miners who lived in these houses also bought for their families from the shops provided. Therefore, the first call on the wages would be rent including electricity, groceries and meat. It was not unusual for a man to go to the colliery office to collect his wages only to be told that there was none for him and in fact he was in debt to the Colliery Owner. I remember one old wag receiving his pay slip one day with all the deductions listed and was not accompanied with any money because he or his family had overspent. He looked hard at the pay clerk and said, "Look, man, you keep my pay and give me the deductions".

Aberpergwm Estate was managed by a man named Spence whose wife was fond of riding horses in the same way as done by a man with her legs across the back of the horse on a saddle made for one of the men. This was of course a very unusual sight particularly in a coal mining village and in this respect Glynneath people were traditional.

Now entrance to the Aberpergwm Estate was not far from the colliery, just off the main road through some beautiful large iron gates near Aberpergwm Church a spot which the majority of men would have to pass on their way home from their day's work at the colliery. Mrs. Spence appeared to have found it convenient to be on horse back just outside these gates at a particular time of the day. She would not dismount to open the gates but would call upon anyone passing at the time to open the gates for her.

I should mention here that it was customary for the Colliery Officials to turn a blind eye to anyone carrying a piece of firewood home from the colliery. But if a man carrying a small piece of wood met on his way home Mr. or Mrs. Spence and on passing did not raise his cap in acknowledgement he would be reported and dealt with at the Colliery office but if he had raised his cap he would have heard no more about it. So if carrying home a small piece of wood in order to help light the fire in the morning it would be better to avoid trouble by the touching of his cap. The Colliery Manager was a Mr. Rhys Howells who apart from being a good mining engineer was very human and took an interest in the welfare of those who worked at the colliery. Whatever happened at the colliery was the business of the manager and would be dealt with accordingly in a very responsible and fair way. But all matters concerning the estate were dealt with by Mr. Spence and there would be trouble for anyone working at Aberpergwm Estate or Colliery who did not acknowledge Mrs. Spence in an acceptable way when meeting her anywhere.

Glynneath was a grand place in which to live, it was about ten miles south of Aberdare and the same distance north of Neath. The Railway Station was about two miles from the village and nearer to the village of Cwmgrach and buses did not start running until the year 1921 so travelling was not very easy. Looking back to the years prior to the 1914-1918 War there was no street lighting and I lived with my parents in a house about three quarters of a mile from the centre of the village. In the winter evenings along with other boys I would go up to the village taking with us a lighted candle in an old glass jam jar in order to give us light to see where we were going. We would then meet as young people in a particular shop and have lots of fun most of our own making. I continued to attend chapel three times on Sunday and at least on one evening every week. The candle and jam jar would always be taken with me when going out from home during the winter evenings and I do not know how I would have managed without them. The boys and girls of the village were a grand crowd and though we had very little entertainment prepared for us we thoroughly enjoyed ourselves in the little shop on the main street. Then came the 1914-1918 War which took away many of our young people who answered the call to

8

fight on behalf of our Country. This made a great difference to the life of the village where the young people were missed in various cultural organisations.

I was in an occupation which exempted me from Military Service but early in the year 1917 a few months after I had attained my eighteenth birthday I volunteered for service and after a short course of training I was sent to Ireland where there was a spot of trouble. The unit with which I served was stationed in about the most westerly part of that little country in County Galway alongside Lough Corrib. I had not been there very long before I was with a number of others selected to go to France and I was told to be ready to move off within a couple of days. When a decision was taken in the British Army in those days it was acted upon almost immediately. I told an Officer that I wanted to have leave of absence for seven days in order to go home and see my family before going abroad on active service. I was indeed quite prepared to go to France but not before having leave of absence. I was informed that my request would not be granted. I then told the Officer that I would not go to France unless I could go home first. He replied we will see to that and he then added that he would be travelling with the party to France.

Well in a couple of days time we left Galway by train on our way to France and we had a roll call on leaving the train and on being transferred to the ferry boat at Dublin and then we had another roll call as we left the boat and went on to the train at Holyhead.

The roll call had therefore been taken on at least two occasions and all had reported correct. I am not aware when the next roll call was taken because a Bill Davies of Colwyn Bay and I had decided to escape at the first opportunity. It was late at night and as we travelled through the darkness the train was going very slowly alongside the coast at Penmaenmawr in North Wales. We jumped out and lay on our stomachs keeping our heads down until the whole of the train had passed by. We then got up and started to walk towards Colwyn Bay but we suddenly remembered that we would have to walk over the Conway Bridge which was at that time guarded day and night, and that there was no way that we could get to Colwyn Bay without crossing that bridge. So we sat down on the side of the road and discussed strategy and decided what to do in case of emergency but in the first place we would walk quietly and yet boldly without making too much noise with our heavy boots, and try to give the impression that we were going home after having a night out. As we got near the bridge we saw light in what was the Guard Room and through the window we could see the guards playing cards. We passed by without any trouble, and on reaching the other side — Llandudno Junction — we gave a sigh of relief and were so very grateful that we were not challenged by the soldiers. On then to Colwyn Bay and a couple of hours rest in Bill Davies's home where I was given a good breakfast before making my journey by train to South Wales and we wished each other the very best of luck. I eventually arrived home at Glynneath and gave my family a shock so I explained to them that I was taking leave of absence before going to France but had to confess that I was doing so against the wishes of my Commanding Officer.

After being home for a day or two I wrote a letter to my Commanding Officer informing him what I had done and that I would report back at the end of my seven days and I would now be prepared to go to France. I kept my word and started my journey back making my way to Fishguard in order to catch the ferry boat to Ireland. All was well until I was about to step aboard at Fishguard Harbour when I was challenged by a Military Police Officer who asked me to produce my papers showing I had been on leave of absence. This of course I could not do and explained that I was returning voluntarily after I had written and given my explanation. He then arrested me and took me to the nearest Police Station which was at Goodwick and not far from the harbour where I was handed over to the Station Sergeant who was told to keep me in custody and await instructions from the Military. I remained there for a few days where I was well looked after and spent most of my time in the living room where I had all my meals with the sergeant, his wife and daughter. In due course an escort arrived from Ireland and on seeing them it could be imagined that I was a very dangerous criminal. To see that I was taken back safely there was a sergeant and a private soldier both properly armed in military style. When we arrived back in Ireland I was placed in custody to await a Court Martial which I attended and gave my defence by explaining very fully what had happened and how I had written to my Commanding Officer explaining that I was now prepared to go to France. I was of course found guilty and sentenced to a period of time in prison and was sent to serve it down in the town of Cork. There I worked in the garden and also at picking oakum, which meant that I was picking old rope to pieces. I had no complaint against the sentence of the Court Martial because I was guilty and prepared to accept the punishment and I do not know how long I was in Cork but I remember being called back and sent to France a much happier person because I had been home for a week. It is strange, is it not, that there are occasions when we take a decision or some action and the result is great satisfaction. That is just what had happened to me and the very fact that I had succeeded in carrying out what I considered to be correct meant a great deal to me and the punishment was taken in my stride. On arrival in France we were taken to a military camp to have a couple of days rest before starting a long march to where the fighting was taking place.

There is one small incident which I would like to place on record, it happened during my early days in France and indeed before I had been in military service all that long. We were in fact a group of young soldiers making our way towards the front line, under the command of a young officer who had himself served in the firing line. Our march lasted a couple of days and as we got fairly near to the front line we took our customary rest alongside the road. The officer addressed us and began by saying, "Young men, you will have no doubt heard many stories from old soldiers of the many battles they had fought and won. My advice to you is that you will not take too seriously all the stories you have heard from old soldiers, but you are now going up to the firing line where you may be called upon to go over the top and face the enemy. If so look around to see if you can see an old soldier anywhere near and if so, hang on to him because his experience will be of tremendous value." This young officer appeared to understand us young soldiers and we got the impression that he knew what he was talking about and also knew of the kind of things we were likely to face when confronted with the enemy in no man's land. This was a lesson for me on the benefits drawn from experience and my thoughts went back to Darran-Du, that little coal mine where I had previously worked and where I, with others, had benefitted when our lamps were burning without giving much light because of the foul air and this was noticed by an experienced miner. The war strengthened my belief in the individual who could if necessary act upon his own and yet could take his place in a team to work with others collectively as was very essential on the battle field.

I was in fact too young to consider all the pro's and con's of the war and why such a war was necessary. I did not go into all the reasons for the war but it was at the time sufficient for me to know that I was fighting for my Country. On my return to civilian life and to a world which was intended to be fit for heroes to live in, I began to think more seriously of how and why the cream of the youth of this Country and of other Countries had been killed in a war which would end wars and make our Country a better place in which to live. I started asking myself many questions such as "Why must there have been a war taking away so many young people? Why could we not be at peace with other Countries and they with us?" These and many other questions caused me much anxiety but I am afraid that they were left unanswered.

I returned to work at Aberpergwm Colliery where I immediately took an active part in the Trade Union and Labour Movement through the South Wales Miners' Federation. I was soon elected to be Vice Chairman of the Miners' Lodge with a membership of more than one thousand.

3

The General Strike of 1926

My election meant that I was a member of the Aberpergwm Lodge Committee which was a very significant organisation in the village because there was no other lodge of such importance and of such influence. As a committee we met in a public house where we had a room set apart for us and in that respect it was quite private. The Miners' Lodge paid for the room in a way that was called a 'Wet Rent' which meant that the cost would be covered by the payment from the funds for two pints of beer per member present. I was young and did not require my share of the beer so the chairman was able to have my beer in addition to his own. This system appeared to work quite well because it gave us privacy and assured the publican of the sale of a number of pints of beer. The Lodge Committee, apart from its work directly concerned with the wages and conditions of the workers at the colliery, was also able to assess public opinion particularly in relation to representation of the electors in local government. When it was time to nominate candidates for a Local Government Election the Lodge Committee would name a candidate to represent Labour and would make its decision known publicly. In the early 1920s this worked quite well and there were no complaints because the Lodge Committee was held in high esteem throughout the village.

This committee work was good training for me as a young man because I was able to put forward my point of view and also I was obliged to listen to what was being put forward by the other members and they were all much older and more experienced than I was. It taught me to excercise tolerance because though I was in a hurry to get things done I often had to concede that other members knew what they were about and were quite sincere.

I was soon involved in the 1921 Coal Miners' Strike and got busy in helping to organise soup kitchens and addressing meetings in an endeavour to keep up the morale of our members and their women folk. In the soup kitchens at Glynneath we were very fortunate to have as cook a man who had been a cook in the army during the 1914-18 war and his services were very much appreciated. At the end of the Strike, we settled to rub our wounds and to start afresh to rebuild our Trade Union into something more influencial and more powerful to face any attack. I attended evening classes taking such subjects as Economics, Philosophy, Socialism, Capital and Labour under such lecturers as Noah Ablett, D. H. Jones, and W. J. Edwards. Noah Ablett was the Miners' Agent in the Merthyr District of the South Wales Miners' Federation and was a very progressive and influential member of the Executive Committee of the Federation. He was a good lecturer and had followed the teachings of Karl Marx and that meant that he was well trained particularly on the subject of economics. I had become a member of the Labour Party which was in those days something more than a political party, it was a Brotherhood, and Socialism was a way of life, with an idealism which went far beyond National Boundary and inspired its members to be prepared to make sacrifices in order to change the system of Capitalism. I also belonged to the Independent Labour Party which was in those days the spearhead within the greater movement. The Socialism preached and practised was very largely built on the Sermon on the Mount. I continued to accept the Christian Faith and remained active within the organisations of the Chapel, and became a Lay Preacher and have retained to this day my faith and my preaching. I have always thought it was such a pity that so many of our people left the Christian Church and Chapel, following the 1921 Strike. They no doubt thought they had been let down by religious leaders. I have always considered the Christian Faith to be a personal matter.

I well remember discussing these things with my father who had been brought up to be a Liberal and read regularly the *South Wales Daily News.* He gave me standards by which to live and repeatedly advised me to never "expect something for nothing but to always give a fair day's work for a fair day's pay". He went on to say that "If you wish to remain active in the Trade Union Movement, then never give any colliery official the opportunity to find fault with your work". I accepted the good advice and acted accordingly. The 1920s proved to be difficult years for the workers in the Mining Industry, wages were low, men were thrown out of work, homes were broken up, dole queues were to be seen in almost every town and village throughout South Wales. In the early twenties, the Aberpergwm Colliery was sold to the Anthracite Combine and this made it much more difficult to represent workers in discussions with the colliery manager because power was taken away from him and he was left with very little freedom to negotiate without making sure that the decision was left to the "Big Man" the agent of the Combine who was in charge of several collieries. They knew that there were men unemployed waiting for jobs held by men now in work and this was used by the employers to their advantage. I remember Lord Buckland (Seymore Berry) waving his stick over my head and saying about himself "I am on the Board of many companies but do not have as much trouble anywhere else as I have in this Colliery".

In about 1924 I went to work for a short time in a colliery in the village of Maerdy (known as Little Moscow) at the top end of Rhondda Fach, ("Little Rhondda"). I was fortunate to find very good lodgings with a lady who was a widow and kept a very good home. Her husband had been a coal miner so she understood the kind of lodgings required by anyone working at the colliery. I worked at number 3 pit and this was the first time for me to be taken down into the mine in a cage because I had previously worked in a level or a drift.

Where I lodged there was another lodger who worked in the same colliery as I worked. He was a member of the Communist Party but I made it clear to him that I could not accept Communism. On arrival home from the pit we would bath in a zinc bath in front of a fire in the middle room of the house. The one who was home first would take off his clothes down to his waist, kneel down in front of the bath and wash the upper part of his body and then the other man would do likewise. When this ritual was completed the one who came home first would take the remainder of his clothes off and step into the bath to wash the remainder of his body. After lodging there for a few days I was the first one home so carried out the first part of the ritual mentioned above. When the time came for me to completely undress and step into the bath I was embarrassed because in the room was the lady of the house and another lady who was a neighbour. I therefore asked the other man to give me a hand to carry the zinc bath to the back room of the house where I would bath. He refused and undressed and stepped into the bath and finished washing himself. The landlady realised the position and took the neighbour out of the room for me to finish washing. That was the last time any female was in the room when I was having a bath. I am sure that my landlady and her friend were not in any way interested in my having a bath but were more concerned with their own conversation!

I did not stay away from home for long but returned and took up employment again in Glynneath in a small colliery named Cwm-rhyd-y-gau, which was part of the Anthracite Combine and where there were above five or six hundred men employed. I was soon elected Chairman of the Lodge which meant the acceptance of responsibility on behalf of the men. Mr. Rhys Howells who had been manager of the Aberpergwm was appointed Agent over several collieries and his brother Mr. James Howells was appointed manager at the colliery where I worked. I could get on reasonably well with both, or either, because I had worked under them and had met them on many occasions when representing the workers at Aberpergwm Colliery. They were reasonable men and understood coal mining and the many difficulties involved but the rat race had begun under the Anthracite Combine and the authority of both men had been undermined. Soon there was another change in the management and a man was brought down from Aberdare who made it clear from the outset that he was in charge and would be the boss. We also had a large number of men from Aberdare and Merthyr working at the colliery, in fact they were much greater in number than the men employed from Glynneath. Industrial relations became very bad because the manager appeared to be determined to cause trouble. I always tried to nip trouble in the bud and would convene pit head meetings to deal with immediate problems, but when it became necessary to fully discuss some difficulty requiring much discussion, meetings would have to be convened in Aberdare, Merthyr, and Glynneath and the votes taken at each of the meetings would be counted and then added together so that the views of all the workers would be known. We had to make sure of a good organisation in order to have full consultation with our members who were living so far apart and found it difficult to stand up to the very aggressive manager without the full support of the committee. With the introduction of the big Anthracite Combine into the Vale of Neath it became necessary for the establishment of a joint committee representing five lodges in order to make sure that not one would feel isolated. We also appointed a full-time agent to look after our interests.

15

Then came the General Strike of 1926 and a number of us got to work immediately in establishing soup kitchens because it meant that the decision to fight against the Coal Owners would mean sacrifice but our cause was just and we were prepared to pay the price. This meant that soup kitchens were brought into being not simply in Glynneath but also in Aberdare and Merthyr to cater for the men who worked in the collieries in Glynneath. The General Strike itself lasted about nine days and then the Miners were locked out by the coal owners who demanded the men to accept a reduction in the very low wages which were then paid to the miners. During the first few days of the General Strike I went along to the railway station which was situated about 2 miles from Glynneath and close to the village of Cwmgwrach. My object was to picket because it had come to our notice that a train was travelling up from Neath every morning bringing a couple of school teachers to Cwmgwrach. The train of course was driven by men known as 'blacklegs' because they were ignoring the decision of the union and playing into the hands of the employers. Along with me on picket duty was a Christian gentleman, the Rev. E. T. Owen, Minister of the Welsh Congregational Church in Cwmgwrach. We could not get near the men who were driving the train because they were on private property but we were on the public highway a little way from the station. We appealed to the teachers who were young ladies not to travel on the train because it was driven by men who were betraying their fellow workers. Our appeal fell on deaf ears and there was nothing more that we could do about it and there was no argument. Some weeks later I was shocked to learn that the Rev. E. T. Owen had been served with a summons to appear before the magistrates in Neath to answer a charge that he had intimidated one of the teachers, and it was alleged that she had been frightened and on arrival at school had fainted. I was the chief witness for the defence because I was the only person on picket duty with the Rev. E.T. Owen. At the trial before the Magistrates, the Rev. E. T. Owen was represented by Mr. Daniel Hopkins who later became Member of Parliament for Carmarthen. He put up a tremendous defence but it was of no avail. The prosecution witness appeared to have thrown all sense of fair play out through the window and went into the witness box and made statements which were glaringly untrue. Alongside the Rev. E. T. Owen I was the only living witness of what happened when those school teachers came off the train and made their way to their place of duty. I am afraid that I was a little naive and did not think that people could be so untruthful when giving evidence on oath. The Magistrates found the Rev. E. T. Owen guilty and called upon him to pay a fine of £20 or go to prison for two months. At the end of the case we went to a cafe in Neath where Mr. Daniel Hopkins took me to one side and informed me that he had seen certain documents concerning my activities which led him to believe that I would be brought before the Court in the very near future. I thanked him for the information and he replied by saying, "If you receive a summons let me know so that I can come down from London to represent you". It is only right to mention here that the Rev. E. T. Owen was a member of the Labour Party and had fought as parliamentary candidate against Alfred Mond in

Carmarthen. I feel convinced to this day that the action of one particular school teacher was responsible for breaking his heart because he too never thought that a teacher who was in charge of children could give such false evidence. He was really shocked and went quietly into the background taking no further part or at least very little in public affairs. I continued my activities on behalf of those with whom I worked and along with the miners in general. I next found myself on picket duty on the public highway near the colliery where I had worked. It had become known that a man who had never worked at the colliery was brought down from Aberdare to work in the engine house. It was my practice to go on picket duty so many days a week and each morning on leaving my home at about 6 o'clock I would be met by a police officer who would ask me where I was going on that particular morning. Sometimes I would give him the information and on other occasions I would not satisfy him but he always made it known that he would be following me. So it was part of my lot to be accompanied by a policeman whenever I left my home early in the morning. One day with the policeman standing alongside of me I spoke to the man who came from Aberdare to work when all the men who had worked at that colliery were on strike. I appealed to him to go back home instead of going to the colliery particularly in view of the fact that he had not previously worked at this colliery. He did not agree to my request and nothing untoward happened: the man went to work and I made my way to the Miners' Office. In a little while a police sergeant came to the Miners' Office. I answered the door greatly surprised when he informed me that I would be reported for trespass and intimidation and then he asked me if I had a statement to make in reply. I must confess that I was completely taken by surprise because I knew that I had done nothing wrong and another police officer had been with me when I spoke to the man who had gone to work. I therefore said to the sergeant, "What I have to say will be said at the proper time and in the proper place". He gave me the impression that he was a little surprised by my reply. I then wished the sergeant and the other police officer good morning. Now my father was a colliery official and was permitted to work during the strike in order to assist in looking after the safety of the colliery not the one where I had last worked but at the Aberpergwm Colliery about a mile and a half away from where I had been picketing. The news was flashed over the 'bush telegraph' to where my father worked and he was informed by another colliery official who expressed his pleasure that I had been at last charged. I was spending most of my time during the days between the Miners' Office and the soup kitchen and during the afternoon I received a message asking me to go home because my father wanted to see me. I immediately went home and my father told me how he had been informed of what was supposed to have happened to me and how I had been charged. He then said to me "What is the charge exactly?" I told him that I was to be reported for trespass and intimidation. "Did you intimidate anyone?" my father asked, I said, "No, I did not". He then said, "Are you telling me that you are completely innocent?" I said, "Yes, father, I am absolutely innocent". He then asked, "What do you think will happen to you?" I replied, "Well if I am taken to court, they will no doubt

17

build up a case against me and in all probability send me to prison". Then the qualities of my father came through when he asked, "Will you face it like a man?" and I said, "Yes, because I have done nothing wrong". He then said, "All right whatever happens I will stand by you", for which I thanked him.

Time dragged on and I continued with my activities on picket duty, in the soup kitchen and addressing meetings in order to keep up the morale of our people. After some time had elapsed I was invited to go to Aberdare to meet the man whom I was alleged to have intimidated and who had now ceased to work at the colliery. The invitation came through an intermediary via Mr. Will Betty our local Miners' Agent who accompanied me to Aberdare to meet the person involved at his home. After some little discussion the person whom we met informed us that attempts had been made to get him to agree to go into a witness box and make certain declarations but to date he had not agreed. He then put forward a proposition to me as follows, "If you will now apologise for what you did by intimidating, I will in return refuse to go into any court and give evidence against you." I said, "I could not apologise for something which I had not done and if I was to apologise it would prove that I had been in the wrong". He got very annoyed and said, "If you refuse to apologise I will be a witness against you". I too got very annoyed and said to him, "Go and do your damnedest. I will never apologise because I did no wrong". I then wished the person "Good night" and along with Mr. Will Betty returned to Glynneath. I was told later that a trap had been set for me but fortunately I refused to fall into it. After some months I learned through the 'grape vine' that the Public Prosecutor had decided that the evidence against me was insufficient and therefore the case was to be dropped. Needless to say this gave me much happiness because I had no desire to become a martyr for a crime which I had never committed. I did not lesson my activities in any way but continued to make sure that my efforts did not come into conflict with the law. The weather during the whole time of the strike was wonderful, just like one long summer. The running of the soup kitchens became a little more difficult because as time went on it was not so easy to acquire the necessary supply of meat and vegetables. However we plodded on determined that one meal a day would be available for our people and we continued to borrow and beg from a variety of places. The small shop keepers were exceptionally good in permitting miners' wives to obtain goods, which could not be paid for, but had faith in the women to pay after the strike would be settled. Anyone writing the history of the strike must in all fairness pay tribute to the person or persons who kept the little shop on the street corner. We also had good friends outside the mining industry who came to our help and supplied money so that we could buy food or in some cases they supplied the food itself. The women had to provide for their children and themselves and the men could have a daily meal at the soup kitchen. There were days when our hearts were lifted by the sight of a ton of potatoes, bags of flour, vegetables, and so on, delivered at the door of the soup kitchen. We set up a committee to be responsible for the running of the soup kitchens and made sure that membership was not to be confined to those on strike. We included the local School Master and one or two Ministers of Religion. Then we had on our staff a cook who had been cooking for the army during the First World War. Apart from preparing all the meals we had to make sure that the place was kept clean and this meant scrubbing the floors. Women were wonderful in the help they gave by scrubbing the floors, washing down the walls, washing clothes, tea cloths, towels and clothes for the cook who did the dirty work.

Some of us went to other parts of the country to those districts not involved in the strike so that we could appeal for food and funds for our own kitchen and indeed for the central fund set up by the South Wales Miners' Federation. One of the places I visited was Hereford and my mode of travel was on the back of a motor bike. In fact there were four of us made the journey leaving Glynneath on a Saturday afternoon, two motor cyclists, and two pillion riders. On our arrival near Hereford we decided to sleep for the night under the hedge of a field. The next morning we went into Hereford and decided it would be advisable for us to report to the Police Station. We explained our mission to a Police Sergeant and to our surprise he informed us that he knew of our arrival, on the outskirt of the city on Saturday evening and he knew where we had been sleeping on that night. In fact he told us that our movements had been checked since we left Glynneath until our arrival at the police station. We left the station and made some enquiries concerning activities in Hereford on a Sunday morning. We were fortunate in meeting a sympathizer who advised us of a meeting of Friends (Quakers) which would be held at Friends' House and he suggested we should accompany him. We accepted the invitation and were surprised to find such a large congregation assembled for the purpose of worship. The one who appeared to be in charge of the meeting invited one of us to give an address by way of an appeal. This fell to my lot and I did my best to explain the position of the miners on strike and of their poverty including that of their families. When I sat down the leader explained that the cause for which I had appealed was worthy of their support. He went on to explain that no doubt many had come to the meeting without sufficient money in their pockets to give to such a worthy cause, and he asked them to place an IOU on the collection plate and the cash could be collected later. This was done and I was assured that a substantial amount was collected. I asked for it to be sent on to the central fund at 2 St. Andrews Crescent, Cardiff. We came away from Hereford very pleased because we had been so well received and found so many people sympathetic to our cause. The strike continued and it is just as well to place on record the great sacrifices made by the miners and their families because in those days to be out of work meant going short of many things. Men and women struggled to keep their heads above the flood of debts surrounding them. They had not been able to save much because they had only just recovered from the 1921 strike and wages were so low. During the strike and prior to it, I was a delegate to the Avon Valley Miners' District Council which met at Aberavon. I was also a delegate to the conferences of the South Wales Miners' Federation held at the Cory Hall, Cardiff, where I usually sat next to the late Aneurin Bevan.

I well remember one conference when Aneurin wanted to speak but could not catch the chairman's eye so he stood up on his chair waving his notes until he was given a chance to address the conference. The South Wales Miners were blessed with leaders second to none in the country and most of them had received very little education but had taken the trouble to become self taught. They were equal to the greatest orators in the United Kingdom and the language used was beautiful to listen to. So many of them had been brought up in the non-conformist Chapel and were fond of making biblical quotations when wishing to make an important point. At these conferences there was invariably a battle going on between those on the platform and those of us on the floor. It was mostly good humoured and in any case it was a wonderful training not only in the art of public speaking but also in the understanding of problems and how they should be approached and overcome. I must confess that I liked attending these conferences because the meeting of delegates from other Colliery Lodges and listening to the addresses from the platform and from the floor gave me some encouragement and helped me not only to keep my belief in the miners but what is also true it helped me to believe in myself.

I would of course not have been able to attend these conferences if it had not been for the help given by my parents who were very wonderful and helped me in every possible way. The Miners' Lodge to which I belonged had spent all its funds and could not collect any contributions during the strike so my parents would pay my train fare to Cardiff and give me sufficient money to pay for a meal. The strike went on and we as members of the Lodge and in particular members of the committee tried very hard to put on a brave face. We not only organised the soup kitchens but brought people together to organise such things as concerts and football matches, I had never before seen a team of women playing soccer against men but this was just one way of providing a little entertainment. Then again we had springing up in the village more than one jazz band and it was great fun to see the way how the bandsmen and bandswomen dressed and the kind of things used for instruments. They brought much relief to a village so hard hit by the strike with no other form of employment available. In order to keep up the morale of our people we saw to it that a lot of entertainment went on in different parts of the village, and regularly meetings would be called in order to keep men and women fully informed of the negotiations which were conducted by our leaders who were in contact with the coal owners. Periodically we would invite all men and women to march through the village in order to demonstrate our solidarity and our determination to keep our ranks closed. I well remember those demonstrations when we were led by a minister of religion riding on a white horse. The demonstrations were always assisted by the singing of our favourite hymns and one in particular was sung to the tune of Cwm Rhondda.

Guide me, O Thou great Jehovah,
Pilgrim through this barren land,
I am weak, but Thou art mighty,

Hold me with Thy powerful hand,
Bread of Heaven,
Feed me now and evermore

Open Thou the crystal fountain
Whence the healing streams doth flow,
Let the fiery, cloudy pillar
Lead me on my journey through;
Strong deliverer,
Be Thou still my strength and shield.

When I tread the verge of Jordan,
Bid my anxious fears subside,
Death of death, and hell's destruction,
Land me safe on Canaan's side;
Songs of praises
I will ever give to Thee.

The effect of the struggle was now to be seen on the clothing worn by men and women, yes and children, because no clothing could be purchased when the bread winner received no wages. It was also getting difficult to keep the soup kitchens going because we had been begging food for such a long time and the sources of supply were unfortunately running out. There were suggestions made in certain quarters that we would have to arrange through our leaders a settlement, or we would be driven back to work because of empty stomachs, and whatever happened we must make sure to remain united and at the same time retain our dignity. The coal owners by their greed were determined to win at all costs, they were vindictive and in my opinion went out of their way to starve us into submission if possible and also destroy the spirit of the coal miners throughout the country.

It is hard to understand why the coal owners were so determined to crush the miners until you realise that they were concerned with profits alone and the miners were simply tools to be used in the production of coal to provide money which would enable the owners to live in luxury whilst the miners lived in poverty. The coal owners in their anger and bitterness throughout the strike did a great disservice to the county, to the miners and to the industry. Coal had been won by the sweat and blood of men who worked under atrocious conditions and long after the strike their sons will remember how their fathers were exploited in the interest of the few.

On the other hand, the result of poverty and the breaking up of homes caused many miners to seek employment in other parts of the country and they remembered how the coal owners had treated their fathers. This I believe strengthened the trade union movement in the years which followed, and indeed to some extent caused many people to join the Labour Party.

4

Dispute

Late in November, 1926 the strike was called off and all men were asked to report back for work in the colliery on December 1st. Some of us understood that *all men* who had worked in the industry prior to the strike would be re-employed so we reported back for work. But obviously the stubborn angry coal owners had other ideas and were going to have their revenge and kick some men when they were down and out. So when I reported to Cwm-rhyd-y-gau Colliery for work I was told "There is no work here for you and never will be in this Colliery or any other Colliery". The owners could not be generous even in their victory and were not satisfied with seeing men suffer almost to starvation, they wanted to drive in the final nail.

I was left with no alternative but to return home and report to the Miners' Agent that there was no work for me at the Colliery. He in turn made appeal after appeal to the coal owners that I should be allowed to return to work and on every occasion the answer was a complete refusal. This was sheer victimisation and at the time very little could be done about it because those negotiating on my behalf were dealing with men who did not understand the word compassion because they considered the miners to be their slaves and treated us accordingly. I therefore applied for Unemployment Benefit but was refused on the grounds that I had turned down an offer of a job digging trenches. Every effort was made by those in charge of the Local Employment Exchange to get me to accept this job away from Glynneath but I knew that if I accepted the job it would mean that I would lose all claim to my work back at the colliery. I was convinced and am still convinced that the Colliery Manager used his influence with the Manager of the Employment Exchange in an attempt to get rid of me. I was therefore determined to fight on and make sacrifices in order to win my case. I continued to apply for unemployment benefit but was always refused. This state of affairs lasted for two and a half years after the completion of the strike so I was without any pay or unemployment benefit for all that time. I was helped by my parents and though it has been said that certain money came from Russia I can assure all concerned that I never received one penny.

Though prevented from working alongside my friends who were back in the colliery, I made a point of visiting the colliery at least once every week for the whole period because I was anxious to keep in touch with the men. I found out that the manager had collected together a few men from Aberdare and Merthyr and persuaded them to form their own non-political breakaway union. This caused me more anxiety and the problem had to be handled very carefully in the hope of retaining the confidence of the majority of those employed at the colliery. I therefore collected the membership subscriptions for the

Cwm-rhyd-y-gau Lodge of the South Wales Miners' Federation. I am glad to say that the men remained loyal and, unknown to the colliery manager, most of the men who were paying to the breakaway union were along with the others paying their contributions to me. During my visits to the colliery I would contact and speak to as many men as possible and very often took the opportunity to address them as they were going to and from the colliery. A non-political union had taken shape in several places in South Wales and a branch was quite near in the village of Hirwain about six miles from Glynneath. Much credit was due to the men whom I represented for their loyalty to the South Wales Miners' Federation much to the dislike of the manager. During my visits I had many a brush with the manager and indeed on one or two occasions with Sir D.R. Llewelyn and Lord Buckland (former Sir Seymour Berry) who were directors and from time to time were supplied with information against me by the colliery manager.

Sir D. R. Llewelyn did not appear to be filled with the determination to have revenge on some of us for our known views and indeed for our actions but I have an idea that he was receiving instructions from faceless men hidden away in some comfortable office. In any case they failed to prevent my visits to the colliery. To meet the men week in and week out was not easy because so many of them were travelling from Aberdare and Merthyr. They were brought down to Glynneath by coaches to a place quite near the colliery premises and then at the end of the shift they would be met at the same place and taken back to their home towns I would therefore go to these points and talk with men as we walked to the mouth of the colliery. The men would arrive at the lamp rooms, collect their lamp and would then take a little break before entering the mine. I would then take the opportunity to address the men before they commenced the day's work and this of course meant me going to the colliery just after six o'clock every morning when I wished to conduct a meeting.

In the Vale of Neath there were five lodges of the Federation representing the men working under the Anthracite Combine, of which Cwm-rhyd-y-gau was one. I had the privilege of being the Secretary of the Joint Lodges' Committee. This enabled me to keep in touch with men working at the other collieries and of receiving progress reports concerning the state of the organisation. This committee repeatedly considered my case and continued to re-build the organisation because the men could not face another dispute with the coal owners until they had recovered from the strike which had sapped away their strength. So the Joint Lodges' Committee could not afford to make any false move so concentrated on rebuilding the organisation and this meant a great deal of effort, strategy and patience before contemplating any sort of confrontation with the employers. Many appeals had been made to the Anthracite Combine but all with no avail and the men throughout the Vale were kept fully informed. However the time arrived when the men felt strong enough to face the consequences of their very reasonable demands but at the same time hoped that the employers would at last be reasonable. It was therefore decided to demand that I should be re-instated at the colliery in which I worked prior to the strike:

24

this was in no way an appeal now but rather a demand. The employers again turned a deaf ear and the miners throughout the five lodges gave fourteen days notice to terminate their contract and refuse to work at the collieries unless I was re-instated.

Every effort was made by our Miners' Agent and others to arrive at a settlement prior to the expiration of the notice given. The last day of the fourteen days' notice had arrived and the owners had not budged. A meeting was arranged between the representatives of the Combine Lodges and representatives of the coal owners. This meeting took place at Maesgwyn House which was used as colliery offices about half a mile down the valley away from Aberpergwm Colliery. In addition to a small deputation for the purpose of conducting negotiations which was led by the senior Miners' Agent for the district, the whole Combine Committee was also in attendance. The deputation only was allowed into the house and all others, of whom there were about thirty or forty men, were in a field outside the house. Fortunately the weather was in our favour and this particular part of the Vale of Neath was then very beautiful and peaceful with its green fields and rows of hedges with the river just below the house flowing quietly down through the valley toward the sea. At intervals the deputation, led by such able negotiators as William Jenkins and John Thomas who were Miners' Agents for the district and Will Betty our local Miners' Agent, along with others from the Combine, would come out to the field and report to the full committee.

The negotiations went on for a number of hours and as can be imagined there were times when members of the committee were getting a little restless. During the early evening we were all provided with a cup of tea and I think we also had biscuits. Again and again we on the outside were consulted on proposals which had been put forward by Sir D. R. Llewelyn who led the representatives on behalf of the coal owners. He was a very astute negotiator and also very determined. I had in the past found him to be fairly reasonable particularly when not influenced by some outside authority. But now he was accompanied by Mr. Rhys Howells, the Agent for the Combine in the Vale of Neath, and also by the manager of the Cwm-rhyd-y-gau Colliery who was known to be the greatest obstacle and it must be kept in mind that he had been brought down from Aberdare to manage the colliery where I worked.

Out in that field with so many of my colleagues I became very confident even though there was so much at stake as far as I was concerned. Readers may ask "Why was I so confident?" The answer is that I was represented by leaders who would fight to the very end in order to secure my return to work. I acknowledged William Jenkins as one of the greatest negotiators of his time and he was supported by others who were negotiating on behalf of men every week and furthermore they were all very loyal and I was content to leave the matter in their hands. I must confess that even in my confidence I was concerned with the ultimate result because if there would be no settlement, then all the miners in the Vale of Neath would be on strike tomorrow and this could cause great poverty for the sake of re-employment of one man.

However late in the evening the representatives of the men came out and the look on their faces was an indication that they had some good news to convey to us. They were very tired but reported that they had been successful, that the notices which had been given by the men would now be withdrawn and work in the collieries would be as usual on the morrow because the owners had given in unconditionally and Cliff Prothero was to be re-instated in his old job at the Cwm-rhyd-y-gau Colliery. Needless to say I was overwhelmed and most grateful to those who had represented me in the negotiations and were not prepared to accept anything less than my right to return to work in the colliery where I worked prior to the strike. I was also very grateful to the whole of the Combine Committee and indeed to all the miners in the Vale of Neath for their loyalty and for their confidence in me. Arrangements were made to advise the workers that their notices were withdrawn and they would therefore go to work tomorrow. Owing to the lateness of the evening there was just one way that the men could be advised of the settlement and the withdrawal of their notices. In those days the method of making announcements was by the use of a Town Crier who would go through the streets ringing a bell to attract attention and then would give the news as he had been directed. I like to think that there was rejoicing in the valley that particular night because common sense had prevailed and a man's right to work had been established. To understand the miners it is necessary to live and work with them, to share their joys and their sorrows. Therefore back to work along with men whom I had known and represented in the past — that was a great experience and one of my first duties would be to convince the men that the break-away union was no use to them and could not represent them in any way. I am glad to state that it was not very difficult because the men rallied around me and the few who were paying their contributions to the non-political union soon ceased to do so and they came into line with the vast majority of the men working in the Colliery.

It was not a happy colliery because the manager who had no doubt been over-ruled during the negotiations concerning my return to the Colliery and he continued to feel bitter. I had to be very careful in every move I took and in everything I said, particularly at the meetings which were held at the pit-head. It was important also for me to put into practice the advice given to me by my father long ago when he said make sure "To do a good day's work for a fair day's pay and never place yourself in a position that any colliery official can criticise your work". Therefore on no occasion did the manager or any other official complain about the amount of work I was doing and its quality. However on more than an isolated occasion I went to the colliery and on reaching the lamp room to receive my lamp before going underground was told, "Sorry your lamp has been stopped". That was the method used by the manager to prevent a man going into the mine, and more often than not it would happen to me when I was working on the night shift. Only a small number of men worked by night carrying out repairs and essential work in the interest of safety. The night shift was due to commence at 11.00 p.m. and on the occasions when my lamp was stopped it meant me returning home late at night after my parents had gone to bed and I would have to disturb their rest and tell them I had been refused permission to enter the colliery and that I had been sacked. This had nothing to do with my work but rather because of some action I had taken on behalf of the men, and on one occasion it was because of what I done as a member of the local authority in publicly protesting against colliery waste being tipped into the river. It is too ridiculous to imagine today but it is an indication of the bitterness maintained by the manager and indeed those in power above him. On such occasions I would ask my mother to call me at five o'clock in the morning for me to go to the colliery and address the men at a pit-head meeting and report to them what had happened to me. The men would give me their support and express their willingness to return home unless I were assured of no further victimisation. Sometimes I would advise the men to go to work and leave the matter to be discussed between the lodge officials and the manager with a view of reaching a settlement. I remember one occasion when my lamp had again been stopped and the men became rather hostile because of the continued attacks on me by the management and therefore the men decided to refuse to work and once again we were on strike. We asked for discussions with the colliery manager but were told that there could be no discussion until the men returned to work. This the men refused to do and after some days discussions took place at the colliery office when there were in attendance representatives of the owners and the miners. The owners were represented by Sir D. R. Llewelyn for whom I had respect because he was a mining engineer and understood what hazards confronted men as they worked in the bowels of the earth. Along with him was Sir Alfred Mond who was a financier and a director of the Anthracite Combine and, of course, also present was the colliery manager. On our side of the table were Will Betty, the local Miners' Agent and myself. During the discussion Sir D. R. Llewelyn, in answer to a question put by Sir Alfred Mond, said, "There is a principle at stake". Sir Alfred, who wanted the man back at work, remarked, "What is that to do with it when we are losing money because no coal is produced?" Well after much discussion a settlement was reached and the men returned to work and I accompanied them.

It would take up a lot of space for me to recount all the battles I experienced with the said colliery manager but time marches on and he returned to Aberdare and we heard no more of him. He was replaced by a Mr. Weaver who was very reasonable and with whom I got on quite well. In fact he would turn to me for advice relative to customs at the colliery and other matters concerning payment to men for special work, and so on. It must be explained here that customs were almost sacred to the miners and they would fight for their retention. The manager had faith in my judgement and in the advice and information which I would give to him. I found him to be very fair in his dealings with men and knew that he would not intentionally do any harm to any workman and I got on with him remarkably well, which for me was a complete change from the past. I was particularly glad of the change because it enabled me to do my work and at the same time continue my activities in public service without the fear of being spied upon by the colliery manager or his representative. The whole atmosphere at Cwm-rhyd-y-gau had been transformed and now we could sit around the table negotiating without any bitterness, not that I could always be satisfied on claims made on behalf of the men but on the other hand I could feel sure of a reasonable settlement. This change at the colliery also meant a great change as far as my home was concerned because I could now go to work and have no fear of being sent home because of my views. My parents never complained but I am sure it must have caused them much anxiety and many sleepless nights — bless them for the support they gave me at all times.

5

Political Office and the Struggle against the
Non-Political Union

In 1929 I was invited to accept candidature for the Neath Rural District Council on behalf of the Labour Party. This was an expression on behalf of the local people, who elected me on my first attempt. The area covered by the District Council reached from Swansea right up to Ystradfellte in Breconshire. It had a population of over forty thousand and was very fortunate to have its own Water Undertaking from which it supplied water to Aberavon and the borough of Neath. It also generated its own electricity and was able to supply electricity to other authorities outside its own area. The Council was in the main anti-Labour on the pretence that as councillors they were independent but in fact they were Tories. A Labour Group was established of which I was appointed its first Secretary and we got down to making the necessary arrangements to be an effective group on the Council. We looked ahead to three years' time when there would be another election and we were determined to win the Council over to Labour. In the meantime we detailed members to take charge of group decisions within the Council Chamber. For example, one would speak on matters of Health, another on Housing, another on Water, another on Electricity, and so on, making sure that every member of the group had a subject which he should study and speak about on our behalf.

The anti-Labour councillors retained all the chairmanships of committees and membership of those committees which they considered important in order to maintain and further their policy.

In virtue of being a councillor I was also a member of the Board of Guardians which covered a much bigger area and had a great deal of work to do because there was so much poverty in the district. There was an understanding between the members and the Relieving Officer, who was himself responsible for carrying out decisions of the Board of Guardians, that in cases of emergency the member would give to an applicant a note to take to a shop in order to obtain food and then the value of the note would be covered to the shopkeeper by the said Relieving Officer and I gave notes on a number of occasions. I can relate numerous stories of people coming seeking notes in order to obtain food. It was all very distressing and certainly depressing to see so many people in dire poverty. There is however one case in particular which even in its poverty provides a slight note of humour. The Relieving Officer, who spoke Welsh, was visiting a house in Glynneath to ascertain for himself some facts about a family requiring extra relief. The husband was much older than his wife and had been home from work for some time suffering from bronchitis. There were a couple of young children in the house and their presence made the Relieving Officer a little curious. He turned to the husband and said in Welsh, "Efe plant chi yw rhein?" and received the reply, "Ie, Ie, chest fi sy'n dost", which translated into English means, "Are these children yours?", "Yes it is my chest which is bad." It is a good story but in English it appears to lose some of its richness of the humour found in the mining districts of South Wales.

As Labour Councillors we prepared for the next local government election at which we succeeded in winning an over-all majority so that we could assure our own nominees of being appointed as chairman of all the committees and making sure that we had a majority of Labour Councillors on every committee. We took as our basis for the election of the chairman of the council seniority, and this appeared to work well so that the senior member of our group was appointed chairman.

In the year 1937 I was elected chairman but that was not all, for when my term of office came to an end, the council re-elected me for the second year. It should be mentioned here that no other Labour Councillor had ever been elected chairman for two consecutive years and this was an indication of the confidence placed in me by my colleagues. Local Government gave me an opportunity to gain a great deal of experience which I value even to this day.

In 1934 there was trouble in several parts of the coalfield created by the activities of the Non-Political Union which came into being following the 1926 strike and was supported by the Coal Owners who had not forgiven the members of the Miners' Federation and were determined to seek revenge. I mentioned the upshot of this Non-Political Union in Cwm-rhyd-y-gau when I was not permitted to return to work after the strike but we did not take long to break it down and to re-organise our own union. The Non-Political Union had spread and appointed a full-time organiser who was assisted in every way by the employers. This caused great concern to the Executive Committee of the South Wales Miners' Federation and they decided to conduct a campaign to combat this break-away union. I was invited to take charge of a district covering an area which included Taff Merthyr and Bedwas Collieries, where the new union appeared to be gaining ground. I therefore went and took up lodgings along with Ted Butler and his wife who lived in Pengam. In Monmouthshire Ted was himself heavily involved in the work with which I was engaged; he was an officer of his branch at the colliery where he worked. Members who were loyal to the South Wales Miners' Federation in the two collieries of Taff Merthyr and Bedwas had come out on strike refusing to work with men who belonged to a union in opposition to their own. Taking control of this district was both difficult and serious because such a large number of men continued to work at these collieries even though some of them did not belong to the new union. Officers of the new union were spending much of their time in this district and at the collieries because they knew they could not hope to win in other districts if they lost here in what was their stronghold. One of our Miners' Agents and a member of the Executive Committee of the South Wales Miners' Federation was Ness Edwards who was completely involved in this confrontation because some of his members were on strike and there were others who had been his members who were now with the new union. This was very distressing for Ness Edwards and others like him who had given such good service to their men and now found that there were those who had turned their back on their own union after the 1926 strike when their loyalty was really needed.

Ness Edwards, by the way, became Member of Parliament for the Caerphilly Constituency in 1939 and served in the 1945 Labour Government. Our leaders in South Wales were conscious that they were now engaged in an unusual kind of fight, where they were being stabbed in the back by men whom they had served who made it extremely difficult because it was like a fight within the family. During the campaign police were available in strength in order to safeguard the renegades as they went to and from the collieries. These people, whom we called 'blacklegs', on leaving the colliery would form themselves into a procession and be escorted by police. Some travelled by train and the police would be there in strength to take them to the railway station and make the necessary arrangements for them to be met at the other end where they would again form a procession and be escorted by police. There would be police in front of them and behind them and again alongside of them so that no one could approach them or get very near to them. They gave me the impression that they were conscious of the suffering they were inflicting upon those who had been their colleagues, they also gave the impression that they were a very frightened lot of people who were afraid to even leave their homes without the aid of police officers. It must have been a very unhappy time for them because though they were working and receiving wages, they were known throughout the whole district as blacklegs and scabs. I considered the men who were on strike were happier, since even though they were not working and received no wages they had the satisfaction of standing by their convictions. Along with other men I would go out early in the morning to meet the men who were taken to the colliery escorted by police and then we would meet them when they came from the colliery again looked after by police.

There was a plot of land near the village of Tiryberth which was a little way below Bargoed, where the men would collect and meetings would be organised with the police near at hand listening to all the speakers and making notes of what was said. I remember one afternoon in particular when we had held a meeting with a very large number of men present. We decided to form ourselves in a procession and walk along the road where we would meet the blacklegs coming from the colliery. We agreed at the meeting that we would be quite disciplined and every person promised that the march would be orderly and in strict silence and when the blacklegs came near us we would all take off our caps and hold same in our hands until the blacklegs and their police escorts had passed. It was felt by us that this form of protest would be a very effective way of expressing our disgust to those men who were betraying their comrades. The march past went off without a word being spoken and our men kept to the agreement and it was considered a big success. We all marched back to the plot of land from where the march had commenced, and again we held a short meeting which I addressed and thanked the men for their discipline and good humour. Ted Butler and I were walking toward his home after the meeting when I was approached by two police officers. Our procession in silence had been too much for them so they told me I would be charged with commiting an offence likely to disturb the peace. I was asked for my name and address which I gave and then I was asked a number of questions which I was not prepared to answer. I informed the police officers that if I was to be charged I would answer questions in the proper place at the proper time. This certainly did not please the police officers. The result of that little conversation was that I was called upon to appear before the magistrates in Bargoed to answer a charge of doing something which was likely to disturb the peace. I was represented by a solicitor named Edward Roberts who later became clerk to the Merthyr Borough Council. The police said many things in the Court which have been forgotten long ago and indeed there would be no purpose in trying to remember them. Edward Roberts put up a really good defence and pulled the evidence of the police officers to shreds in the presence of the Chief Constable who made a point of being present in the Court. The magistrates, however, in their wisdom and which was no doubt to them in the interest of justice believed the police officers and I was called upon to pay a fine of £5.

That was not the end of my trouble during the campaign because I kept addressing meetings throughout the district including the towns and villages where some of the blacklegs lived. I also visited several collieries and addressed pit-head meetings and to my great surprise I was served with a Writ seeking an injunction to prevent me ever setting foot again upon the premises of one particular colliery in that district. The Order was served upon me with a demand that I was to pay the court costs: this was like trying to draw blood out of a stone. I therefore appeared before a meeting of the Executive Committee of the South Wales Miners' Federation in Cardiff when my good friend Jim Griffiths was in the chair. After I explained the position Jim told me to forget about it, the matter would be taken over by the Executive Committee.

After a long drawn out struggle the battle was won by the South Wales Miners' Federation and the Non-Political Union in South Wales was compelled to fold up. This has not been a very pleasant feature to record because it is one thing to fight against the Coal Owners but quite another matter to fight against men with whom you had worked in the colliery. It has taken many years for the bitterness to be forgotten in places like Bedwas and I fear that the effects of that struggle still crop up in discussion with the local people. I returned to Glynneath and back to the colliery to follow my employment and to continue to represent members of the Cwm-rhyd-y-gau Lodge.

6

The Delegation to the Soviet Union

In 1936 I was appointed by the South Wales Miners' Federation along with three other members to take part in an International Trade Union Delegation to visit Russia. I with the other members of the delegation spent six weeks in the Soviet Union which I found to be very interesting, though I must confess I was also a little surprised and was not too favourably impressed. I was invited to give a talk on the radio from Moscow which was transmitted to many parts of the world including Great Britain. I had in the first place to submit a script to be considered by the appropriate authority and this was understandable but when it was returned to me I hardly recognised it. The things I wanted to say had been crossed out and a great deal of blue pencil had been used. I picked up the pieces and gave the talk or at least that part of the script which had been authorized and it was heard here in South Wales.

During one of our many conferences held with leaders of the Soviet Union for our benefit every word spoken by the delegates from different parts of the world was translated into a number of languages. One of our delegates from South Wales in the person of Tom Andrews from Treharris stood up and started to address the conference in Welsh and interpreters were amazed and could not understand what was happening, until one of them came to me and asked what language was being spoken. I said Welsh and the interpreter and others joined me in a smile but we had to be careful not to offend and this could so easily have happened. Much has happened since 1936 not in Russia alone but indeed throughout the whole world and I would like to have returned to the Soviet Union to see what changes have been made and what progress has taken place following their hard struggle.

Prior to my going to Russia and indeed throughout my life up to that time many approaches had been made to me with a view of me joining the Communist Party. In fact when I was victimised following the 1926 strike, a friend came along and said that he was in a position to offer me a job as organiser with the Communist Party. I turned the offer down even though for some time the coal owners and their representatives had said in no uncertain terms that I was a Communist. However, I could never bring myself to believe that Communism was what was required in this country. I found out from men who worked alongside me that they too often carried out directives given from the Head Office of the Communist Party.

During our six weeks in Russia we travelled wide and far from Leningrad to Moscow, down to the Don Bas and then to Sochia holiday resort on the Black Sea. I have already mentioned the name of one delegate from South Wales and the other two were Will Arthur, who later became Secretary of the South Wales Miners' Federation, and Jim Grant who was agent for the mechanical workers who had their branches with the Federation. The four of us from South Wales did all we could to keep together on organised visits to schools, hospitals, collective farms, factories and coal mines and the four of us knew a little about the latter. The Stakhanovite movement was taking shape in every industry and this meant that those who produced more than what was known as the 'norm' would be given presents for their extra efforts. We were not very impressed but agreed that it might serve a purpose in Russia at that particular time, though we were very sure that this kind of movement would not be acceptable in Wales. It gave an advantage to the strong over and above the weak and we thought it was the first duty of the State to look after those who were less able to fend for themselves.

We spent some time down a pit at the coal face discussing with the management the method of coal-getting and at one stage Will Arthur and I were invited to accept jobs in their mining industry. Needless to say we made it clear that we could not entertain any offer but at the same time expressed our thanks. Leaving behind the mining industry we made our way down to the Black Sea and after much travelling we arrived at a little place called Sochi and we were taken to a large hotel which was reserved for holidays for Red Army Officers. It was a most luxurious place with a menu on the dining table that appeared to offer meals more elaborate than I had ever seen before. We delegates were treated very well on the social side, our meals were good and gave no indication of shortage. The Russians who were looking after us were of course in a very favourable position and this was quite understandable because we knew how any representatives of a foreign country were treated when visiting Britain and this would also apply to those who were acting as guides. Most of our evenings were arranged for us and great care was taken regarding the places where we would have dinner. On such evenings we would commence eating at about 8.00 p.m. and would be eating and drinking at 2.00 a.m. the following day. They had a custom of taking one course then having a smoke or a walk along the dining room and that was not all, they would arrange for Toasts to be moved between the courses, and many speakers took part. Every effort was made to convince us of the benefits of Communism and to their surprise some of us were not easily convinced. I should point out that the four delegates from South Wales caused some difficulty because a special report was prepared which laid much emphasis on the way the delegates were impressed on all they had seen. We were asked to sign the report so that it could be published with our support. But the four of us refused to add our names unless we were permitted to amend parts of what was in the report. This led to some controversy and much pressure was used with a view of securing our signatures in order that the report would be made known to the trade union movements of the countries represented by delegates of this World Trade Union Delegation.

On leaving Russia we were again joined by a man named Ralf Fox who was a journalist and an important member of the Communist Party and though he had travelled out on the same boat as us we did not see much of him during our six weeks in the Soviet Union but here he was once again on the same boat coming home. He had taken part in the Spanish Civil War and was no doubt thought a lot of by leaders of the Communist Party. It may sound strange but he had with him on the boat leaving Russia a copy of the report which we had refused to sign and he tried very, very hard to get us to sign but all his efforts were of no avail.

Much of what we had seen meant that a great deal had been achieved under difficult circumstances, yet on the other hand there were things to which we could not give our approval. The attitude taken by Ralf Fox on our return journey convinced us then that he was on the ship going out and again on the ship coming back not by accident but rather by a carefully arranged plan. However he received our replies in no uncertain terms. It was the first Trade Union Delegation for which no official report was published and this all because four members of the South Wales Miners' Federation were not prepared to add their signatures to things which they did not believe.

I think that some of my friends thought that my visit to the Soviet Union would result in my joining the Communist Party but this was not so and in fact I came back more convinced than ever that Communism was not a way of life for me.

7

Experience in Public Service

In 1937 I married Violet Elizabeth Thomas, daughter of Llewelyn and Rowena Thomas of Pontardulais. Vi to date had a very sheltered life and was non-political, but soon became involved in the Labour Party and gave much of her time and energy working on behalf of the Party and I shall for ever be indebted to her for the way she sacrificed so much and spent so much time alone at home, thus enabling me to continue with my activities in the trade union and Labour Movement. I was then checkweigher at the Cwm-rhyd-y-gau Colliery working for six days per week for a wage of £3. I had been elected to this post at a secret ballot of all the men who worked at the coal-face. There were about ten applicants for this job and I was fortunate enough to win on the first ballot by having more votes than all the other applicants put together. However when the result was reported to the Lodge Committee a certain person who was friendly with one of the applicants, who was a member of the Communist Party, asked that a second ballot should be held between the communist applicant and myself to determine who should be elected. This was ruled out of order by the Committee because the ballot was so decisive and the attempt made for a further ballot was obviously wrong and the member who raised the matter was put in his place. My job as checkweigher did not affect the day wage men but only those who were actually producing coal and were paid a rate for every ton brought to the surface and screened. My job was to check that the man who weighed the coal on behalf of the company put the correct weight in the book provided. When a tram of coal came on to the weighing machine, the gross weight would be taken, then the weight of the tram itself was deducted. Then the tram would be tipped so that its contents would pass over a screen and all the small coal would run down between the bars into what was called a Billy Box, and the weight in that box would be shown on a big clock. That weight would then be taken away from the gross because the collier would not be paid for the small coal that went through the screen into the 'Billy'. The Company weigher would then enter all this information in his book and I would enter it in my book. Each collier was given a number which he would chalk on the tram before it left his place of work and this would enable the weigher and me to know to whom to credit the amount. At the end of the week my book would be checked against the weigher's book and then on the Monday morning I would issue a weight slip to each individual collier for him to know the tonnage of coal for which he would be paid. I enjoyed my work and had very little spare time because in addition to my trade union work and my membership of a local authority I was also helping in propaganda campaigns on behalf of the Labour Party. I can well remember one occasion going to Pembrokeshire along with two friends, Mr D. T. Jenkins Skewen and Mr D. R. Grenfell, MP for the Gower Constituency. We went to help the then Parliamentary Labour Candidate, Billy Jenkins of Hoplas Farm who was known throughout the Labour Movement because of his many activities and of his sacrifices in the cause of Socialism. Billy was a well known pacifist and though this was not very acceptable in a place such as Pembroke Dock, he himself was very popular in other parts of the county and was a great character. In fact it was Billy Jenkins and men and women of his calibre who were responsible for the building of the Labour Party. When Mr Desmond Donnelly won Pembrokeshire for Labour, I remarked that the credit belonged to the little man from Hoplas Farm who had for years sown the seed and cared for it in such a way that made it possible for those who followed to reap the harvest. All our supporters in the County of Pembrokeshire should raise their hats in honour of the unselfish Billy Jenkins who worked so hard in and on behalf of a cause in which he believed so much.

On our visit to Pembrokeshire, we spent a couple of days addressing meetings and covering a number of towns and villages talking to people and spelling out the reason of our visit. It was D. T. Jenkins who used his car on this and on many occasions for the purpose of taking speakers to and from meetings. At the end of our tour I had to get back to Glynneath in time to go to work at 7 o'clock in the morning, so after addressing a meeting in Fishguard late in the evening we made our way back and I got home about 3.00 a.m. which enabled me to have a couple of hours sleep before going to the colliery. Those were exciting times and no amount of sacrifice appeared to be too great in the hope of bringing about a state of affairs in which our idealism would be satisfied.

Life was hectic but enjoyable particularly when working for a cause to enable equality of opportunity for all and we are still aiming toward that goal. From 1937 I was an *ex officio* Magistrate in my capacity as chairman of the Neath Rural District Council and then in 1939 my name was added to the Commission meaning that I became a Magistrate in my own right. There was no payment in those days, not even travelling expenses for attending meetings in connection with the Local Authority nor indeed for attending to my duties as a magistrate. I simply mention this because the distance from Glynneath to Neath was ten miles and that meant I had to pay return bus fare for meetings I attended and for every time I sat in court. This happened to all councillors and magistrates. Attending the Court or a meeting was not all because more often than not it would be necessary to have a meal and this was extra expense, but anyone accepting appointment as a Magistrate, or nomination for the Council, would know what was involved and there were no complaints. There was much enthusiasm in voluntary service and those engaged therein had a certain amount of satisfaction in the knowledge that they were helping people who were in need of help.

There was a woman in our village who came to see me very often seeking more relief than she had been given by the Relieving Officer. Just after I had married and was living in a small semi-detached house, and my wife was new to the district, to the people and to politics, a woman called at the house along with a dog and enquired for me. I had not arrived home from the colliery and my wife explained that I would, when I came home, hurry over my meal and rush to catch a bus for Neath in order to attend a meeting of the Local Authority. The woman then said "I will sit on the door step, until he comes home because I must see him." My wife therefore invited her and the dog into our home and I leave it to you to imagine what it was like for my wife, having just got married and trying to prepare a meal with a strange woman in the house, who kept walking with the dog around the table, because the dog kept barking. We had a little dog of our own but my wife had to place it in the bathroom and close the door in order to avoid a fight, but the continual barking of the two dogs did not help my wife in any way! On my arrival I had to sit down and listen to the complaints from our visitor and I can assure you that she made it all very complicated. I decided to get in touch with the Relieving Officer in Neath that very afternoon and that is just what I did. The woman on leaving my home assured my wife that she was quite accustomed to coming to me for help. My wife by this time was very worried and wondered what sort of a meal she had prepared for me, but it worked out really well and I enjoyed it and then rushed out of the house to catch my bus. Receiving callers at my home requiring help was just what was to be expected when I was engaged in public life and I had experienced this kind of thing for a number of years but it was quite strange to my wife who took a little time to understand the reason for some of those who called. In those days a local councillor was expected to be more than a representative: he was looked upon, and made use of, as an adviser on all kinds of subjects, and also an advocate, a letter writer, and an information bureau without the aid of any office facilities. I was also at that time Secretary of the Neath Constituency Labour Party and Election Agent to the then sitting Labour Member of Parliament, William Jenkins, whom I had known for many years and who was in charge of the negotiations which resulted in my return to the colliery after being victimised following the 1926 strike. I was pleased to be associated with him because I acknowledged his experience and his integrity and from him I learned a great deal in the affairs of local government and in the art of negotiation. Neath Constituency was then a safe labour seat, though we had not had a General Election since 1937, and following the death of William Jenkins, the Labour candidate at the by-election polled 39,947 votes against 12,000 for the opposition. It is only fair to point out that there was a political truce between the big political parties because of the war. This meant that if a seat had been held by Labour there would be no opposition from the Tories and the Liberals at the by-election, but this did not prevent splinter parties putting up candidates. This is just what happened when the Welsh Nationalists and the Revolutionary Communists decided to contest the seat. I well remember when all the votes were counted and it was obvious that the Labour Candidate, D. J. Williams, had retained the seat, the Welsh Nationalist Candidate, Mr Wyn Samuel, came over to me and asked what were his rights concerning his making a request for a re-count. I not only advised him to approach the Returning Officer but made it clear that I would support his request. In order to understand his concern it is necessary for me to mention that each candidate deposits the sum of £150 with the Returning Officer when nominated and in order to have this sum of money returned he would have to poll one eighth of the total votes cast in that election and Mr Samuel was doubtful whether he had polled sufficient. The Returning Officer agreed to check over the bundles in order to make sure that no votes had gone into the bundles of a candidate to whom they did not belong. Anyhow the result of this by-election was that the Welsh Nationalists saved his deposit but the Revolutionary Communist lost his. The Neath Parliamentary Constituency was made up of three local government areas, Neath Borough, Neath Rural and Pontardawe Rural, all under the control of Labour Councillors. My political activities went far beyond the locality in which I lived, and in 1937 I was very interested in the setting up of a Regional Council for South Wales with the full support and backing of the Trades Union Congress and the National Executive Committee of the Labour Party. This new body was made up of all sections of the Trade Union Movement and Labour Party throughout the whole of South Wales. It really came into being as a result of propaganda conducted by the Communist Party and their infiltration into certain sections of our Party. George Morris, who was then Organiser of the Labour Party for Wales, called together about a dozen reliable members of the Labour Party along with several trade union officers to discuss creating the Regional Council. I was privileged to be one of a small group with the responsibility of drawing up recommendations for the rules and constitution which were later submitted for acceptance to a conference. There were one or two trade unions, where the Communists had some influence, which were very much against the new organisation and perhaps for the very simple reason that according to our rules and constitution no member of the Communist Party, the Fascist Party, the Tory Party, or the Liberal Party, could attend any of our conferences, neither could they be delegates to our conferences. This, as was expected, intensified activities in certain quarters against the Labour Party and particularly on a constituency level, where I have to confess that much infiltration had taken place. By this time I was also Secretary of the Glamorgan Federation of Labour Parties and also a member of the Executive Committee of the new organisation, the South Wales Regional Council of Labour. In 1939 the Second World War came upon us. This placed a tremendous strain upon the Labour Party, and on the trade union movement in particular, because its favourable conditions for communists and other fifth columnists led disgruntled people to work against the Labour Movement. It also brought about some hardship and much anxiety, but in a variety of ways it brought people together through working in one or more of the many voluntary organisations all helping in the War Effort such as Air Raid Wardens, Fire Watching, First Aid, Demolition Squads. All these and other services brought men and women away from their homes to give of their service in co-operation with others and in the interest of our country. In order to make the best possible use of services and material the country was split up into Regions and though there were many committees appointed to co-ordinate the services, there was also a Regional Commissioner: for South Wales, he was Sir Gerald Bruce, Lord Lieutenant of the county of Glamorgan, with whom I got on exceptionally well.

During the year 1941 we were in great danger of being invaded and arrangements had to be made for any kind of contingency. Sir Gerald Bruce would be in complete control of operations as far as civilians were concerned. Our Courts had to be prepared to deal with such things as looting and the many other kinds of crime that usually accompany an invasion. Therefore arrangements were made to set up War Zone Courts under the Emergency Powers (Defence) Regulations 1939-40 and South Wales was to be one of the War Zones. A small number of magistrates were appointed to sit with a Judge in the Special Courts held anywhere in South Wales. I was appointed as one of the magistrates and supplied with information concerning the powers of the Courts and the name of the Judge for our Zone. In my letter of appointment I was informed that the Courts would not come into being until there was an order made by the Home Secretary and he would act according to the circumstances if the enemy reached any part of our Country. Looking back I am now able to consider it to have been a great honour to have been appointed one of a small number to sit with a Judge in a Court with such great powers. On the other hand, I am indeed very grateful that we were not invaded and therefore the Court was never called upon to exercise its powers. To this day I have not been informed of the withdrawal of the Regulation neither have I been informed of the cancellation of my appointment. The correspondence in connection with my appointment is now deposited in the archives of the Glamorgan County Hall, Cardiff, but for those who are interested I herewith include copies..

STRICTLY PRIVATE
H/Wms

25th July, 1941.

HENRY ROWLAND
Clerk of the Peace and
Clerk of the County Council

Dear Sir,

WAR ZONE COURTS,
Emergency Powers (Defence) Acts, 1939-40

You may be aware that under the powers of the above Acts, regulations have been made by the Secretary of State which will enable War Zone Courts to be established for the purpose of securing the trial and punishment of offenders in any place in which, by reason of recent or immediately apprehended enemy action, the military situation is such that Criminal Justice cannot be administered by the ordinary Courts with sufficient expedition These Courts will not come into being until a particular area has been declared by an Order of the Minister of Home Security to be a 'War Zone'.

For the purposes of these Courts, a special panel of "Advisory Members" is being recruited from among the Justices of the country, and the object of this letter is to inquire whether you would be prepared to act upon this panel if I submit your name to the Secretary of State.

The War Zone Courts will be presided over by the President (a High Court Judge) and two Advisory Members, but there will, for certain purposes, be local Courts when two Advisory Members may sit without the President for certain administrative functions and when acting as a Court of First Instance.

The Justices comprising the Panel will not be entitled to sit unless they have been specially "appointed" by the President to sit with him or directed by him to sit in his absence. Although these Special Justices will probably have jurisdiction over the whole of the South Wales Region — consisting of the Counties of Brecknock, Cardigan, Carmarthen, Glamorgan, Monmouth, Pembroke and Radnor — it is intended that ordinarily they will act locally so that the Courts may have the benefit of their local knowledge.

I have been appointed to be the Clerk to the War Zone Courts for the South Wales Region and therefore I should be glad if you would let me know whether you are prepared to allow your name to be submitted to the Secretary of State for appointment to the special panel of Justices for the South Wales Region.

I enclose stamped addressed label for your use.

I am,
Yours truly,

Clerk of the Peace

Clifford Prothero, Esq., J.P.
The Nook,
Woodlands Park,
Glynneath, Glam.

PERSONAL

HENRY ROWLAND
Clerk of the Peace and
Clerk of the County Council   17th November, 1941
Dear Sir,

WAR ZONE COURTS,
SOUTH WALES DISTRICT

I am requested by the Hon. Mr. Justice Lewis, the President of the War Zone Court for the South Wales District, to say that he had appointed you to act as an Advisory Member of the Court or any division thereof when sitting within the geographical County of Glamorganshire or in an adjoining County.

The Court will not be set up till the South Wales District or any part thereof is declared to be a War Zone by Order of the Minister of Home Security, and your appointment will become effective from the date of such order and will be for the whole period that the South Wales District or any part of it is declared to be a War Zone. The Regulations require the presence of two Advisory Members at any sitting of the Court, and notice will be given to you when your attendance is desired. The President will do his best to ensure that the burden of attendance is fairly distributed among the Members of the Panel.

Any alteration of address or resignation occurring during the continuance of the war, should be notified at once to me at the above address.

I should be obliged by your acknowledging receipt of this letter to me on the enclosed form.

Yours faithfully,

C. Prothero, Esq.,
The Nook,   Clerk of the War Zone Court
Woodlands Park,   for the South Wales District.
Glynneath, Glam.

WAR ZONE COURTS
SOUTH WALES DISTRICT

I the undersigned President of the War Zone Court established for the South Wales District * in pursuance of the powers conferred upon me by Regulation 3 of the Defence (War Zone Courts) Regulations 1940, HEREBY APPOINT the Justices of the Peace whose names appear as Members of the Panel of Advisory Members, constituted by a Secretary of State, for the said District to act when required as Advisory Members of any War Zone Court for the said District or any division thereof.

I HEREBY DIRECT that any two Members of the said Panel shall sit in my absence as a War Zone Court for the said District, for the purpose of exercising any power which under the said Regulations or the War Zone Court Rules 1940, such a Court has jurisdiction to exercise in the absence of the President.

The above appointments and directions shall be effective from the date of any Order made by the Minister of Home Security, declaring the South Wales District to be a War Zone and shall continue in force during the whole time that the said District continues to be a War Zone.

DATED this 17th day of November, 1941.

President of the War Zone Court
for the South Wales District

* Consisting of the geographical Counties of Brecon, Cardigan, Carmarthen, Glamorgan, Monmouth, Pembroke and Radnor.

In the early part of the War, Cwm-rhyd-y-gau Colliery was closed down because the seam of coal was too expensive to work and I took up a temporary job as Chief Billeting and Welfare Officer in connection with the mothers and children who were evacuated to our district from areas near London where there was much bombing. The job was very interesting and also very exacting particularly in dealing with the women who fortunately were much less in number than the children. We requisitioned a large house in Cadoxton where all the women could be housed together under supervision, which was necessary because with a number of women coming into our area from different parts of the country and with different backgrounds. In billeting the children, the problem was not so great and in the main it was not difficult to place the children in homes where they were given a warm welcome and affection.

On arrival home very late one night my wife said "Go upstairs and you will find a little girl who has been billeted with us. She is very frightened and said she would not go to sleep until you came home." Upstairs I went and there tucked up in bed was the little girl, obviously very nervous and her little face was quite white. She told me her name was Peggy Carcas and she lived in Gillingham, Kent. Her two sisters were billeted in another home not far away.

43

Peggy was about eleven years of age and her parents remained at home but agreed that it was better for the children to be taken to a safer district. My wife and I, having no children, took to Peggy on first sight and treated her as if she was our own and for this we have no regrets.

Peggy's mother and father came down on more than one occasion to see Peggy and her sisters and we kept them informed of the children's welfare. Peggy came to a Welsh Congregational Church named Capel-y-Glyn with us and learned sufficient Welsh to enable her to take part in the services. Eventually Peggy went back home, found herself a job and settled down. My wife and I were invited to her wedding and were very thrilled and excited. Peggy looked lovely as a bride and the boy she married was and still is a grand fellow. It is now a long time since the early part of the war when children were evacuated from their homes, but time does not appear to alter our relationships in any way because we have kept in touch throughout the years. Peggy has four children, one of them is married and they all come down to see us once or twice every year and, believe me, their visits are much appreciated. The short time that she was with us in Glynneath, she really became the central attraction of our home. She would deal with visitors and take telephone calls, and when callers would ask over the telephone, "Who is speaking, is it Mrs Prothero?" Peggy would answer, "No, I'm Uncle Cliff's little girl". I never discussed politics with her but she knew of my involvement and during the 1945 General Election she went to the Labour Party office in her home town and took on voluntary work as a typist. As I now sit back looking over the years that are gone and re-counting my blessings which have been many, I include in them Peggy, and not only the time she spent with us in Glynneath, but also the friendship over the many years which is as real today as ever it was.

8

Labour Party Officer

In 1942 the Labour Party advertised the full-time post of Organiser in the Eastern Counties. This post had been held by Mr Morgan Phillips who had gone to work in Transport House, Headquarters of the Labour Party, and later became General Secretary. The post now advertised, had been vacant for some time and probably the War had something to do with this. The post of Organiser was generally considered to be promotion for one who was a full-time agent in some part of the country. I learned that on one occasion only had an appointment of this kind gone to a person who was not already a full-time agent and that was in Scotland. However, after a lot of thought, I decided to make an application and went on to complete an application form. I was placed on a short list and decided to talk the matter over with Mr George Morris who was full-time Organiser for Wales and who was a first class officer with whom I was very friendly. George gave me encouragement and advised me to go forward in confidence and said "Remember, Cliff, when you appear for interview before the appropriate sub-committee of the National Executive Committee, that you know more about organisation than any of those members". I was afterwards told that a fellow Councillor was heard to remark, "Cliff has applied but he stands no chance at all."

On my arrival in London for the interview I soon realised that I was up against stiff opposition, for all the others appearing on the short list were full-time agents and, of course, I was not. These men had been in their posts for some years and had served the Party well but to make things a little more difficult one of the applicants was the full-time agent in a constituency where the Member of Parliament was none other than Mr Herbert Morrison. It so happened that my interview took longer than any one of the others and I was not quite sure what to make of the length of my interview.

The General Secretary of the Labour Party was then Mr Jim Middleton who expressed the view that I was needed in the House of Commons and then asked me, "Would you not prefer to be a Member of Parliament?" I replied, "No, because I wish to be an Organiser." The chairman was Mr George Ridley, and other members of the committee included Jennie Adamson, Alf Dobbs and George Shepherd, the then National Agent (who later became Lord Shepherd). To be interviewed was a new experience for me, because the other posts which I had held had been by election. It was a thorough interview carried out by men and women who had given long and faithful service to the Labour Movement. When all short listed applicants had been interviewed we were informed that an appointment had been made and each one of us would be informed in writing.

We, the applicants, left Transport House and went together to have some refreshments in a nearby public house. One of the applicants gave the remainder of us the benefit of his knowledge by dropping a bombshell in our midst. He said that the interview had been a bit of a farce because it was known before we came to London that the appointment had been made and he was the successful applicant. We congratulated him and raised our glasses to his success and wished him all the best in his new post. Before we parted he turned to me and asked if I would like to apply for the post of full-time agent which he would now be vacating. I replied by saying that I would not apply but would continue to serve the Movement in a voluntary capacity. Then I went off to meet my wife who had come to London along with me because I promised her that we would spend a night in the big City. I told her all that had happened and she said, "Come along, let us enjoy ourselves," and appealed to me not to be too disappointed.

My wife and I then went off to the House of Commons to let Sir William Jenkins, Member of Parliament for Neath Constituency, know the result of the interview because I knew he would be interested and of course he was concerned with my well being. This would be a new experience for my wife who had never been inside the House of Commons. On arrival I sent a note into our Member of Parliament who came out immediately and took us to a room and gave us tea. I then explained to him what had happened and how all the other short listed applicants were full-time agents and probably the fact that I was not one held against me. I explained how we had collected together after the interview and congratulated the successful applicant, we were all good friends and there was no bitterness over the appointment and now I would be remaining with him in Neath. He then took us along to the Chamber of the House of Commons where we were fortunate to be provided with seats usually reserved for special guests: this was during the War and certain parts of the House had been closed. Sir William resumed his seat which was not very far away from where we were sitting so we were in a position to see and hear the Members of Parliament. After being there some little time, Mr Alf Dobbs, one of the members of the committee that interviewed me, and who was a Member of Parliament, spotted me, came over and asked very quietly if I had been told what happened following the interview. I said that I had not been told anything officially but Mr George Shepherd informed me with the other applicants that we would be advised of the appointment in writing. Mr Alf Dobbs then said, "Oh well, I can tell you that you have been appointed and George Shepherd will be inviting you to meet him in order to discuss certain matters that will need immediate attention." I was really dumb-founded and did not reveal to him what had happened in the public house when another man had been congratulated. I thanked Mr Dobbs. I then found a way to let Sir William Jenkins know that I again wished to speak to him. I succeeded in meeting him outside the Chamber where I informed him what had happened. Sir William Jenkins of course knew Mr Alf Dobbs very well and was very pleased with the news. He congratulated me and gave me a big cigar to enjoy that evening. I could not help thinking about what had happened in that little public house after the interview. I began to feel very sorry for one who had convinced himself that the job was his and who would now feel very disappointed: it must have been a terrible blow to him and to his pride. As time went on, he and I became good friends and neither of us ever mentioned the incident to one another or indeed to any one else.

In due course a letter arrived from Mr George Shepherd informing me that I had been appointed and inviting me to meet him in a large house in the country which had been taken over by NATSOPA, one of the printing trade unions, which could be used for special purposes by the Labour Party. George Shepherd was a very efficient National Agent and knew how to get the best out of people without making use of his authority in any way. During our discussion he handed me an old shoe box which contained a number of cards with the names and addresses of Labour Party Secretaries who had held office prior to the out-break of War. That was the total equipment supplied for me to go and organise in a district which was completely strange to me. Later on, I received through the post some report forms and sheets so that I could indicate my expenses. I was to live in Cambridge and organise the whole of the Eastern Counties from this one centre. This meant me buying a second hand eight horse power car, in which I was given a few driving lessons by a friend of mine. I then drove from Glynneath to Cambridge: there were no driving tests during the War. That drive meant my going through strange country and along many roads without any help from signposts because none were in use. My appointment made it necessary for me to arrange for accommodation in Cambridge, where I knew no one and no one was known to me. Fortunately arrangements were made through correspondence for me to have accommodation with Mr and Mrs Patterson, who were very active members of the Labour Party. Mr Patterson was also the secretary of the local Trades Council and Labour Party, as well as secretary of his trade union branch.

Mrs Patterson was a very good cook and on Sundays served a large portion of Yorkshire Pudding as a first course. Then we would have the usual meat and vegetables followed by a sweet and tea or coffee. I considered myself particularly fortunate in having such good digs where the fullest possible use could be made of the ration book. I soon made a number of friends including a Percy Dennard who was a County Councillor but, what was perhaps more important, he once worked on the railway in West Wales and was a good Socialist. He, with his wife, one son and four daughters lived in Campbell Street, where I was able to call at any time. I accepted their kind hospitality and I called upon them very often, but as I entered the house the kettle would be placed on the fire and tea and some eats would be prepared in a very short time. They were a delightful family and I will never forget their kindness to me, a stranger in their midst, and I am glad to exchange greetings with one of the daughters at least every Christmas. Cambridge itself was much different to the mining valleys of South Wales and members of the Labour Party in this centre of learning gave the impression that they were above the ordinary manual workers. Prior to attending my first meeting of the Trades Council and Labour Party, I was advised not to mention the fact that I had been a coal miner in South Wales. This to me appeared to be an indication that they did not think much of the men with whom I had received my political training and my education. Well, I turned up at my first meeting, which was well attended by delegates from a variety of organisations. The Chairman gave me a very warm welcome and made a point of saying what was expected of me in my capacity as Organiser. He went on to say that I too, like Mr Morgan Phillips their previous Organiser, came from South Wales. In response I thanked the Chairman for his cordial welcome and for the very kind way the meeting received me in their midst. I decided that if there was to be any encounter between the local Labour Party and me it was just as well to clear the decks at my first meeting. I went on to say that I was pleased to be in such a place as Cambridge and I wanted them to know that not only had I come from South Wales, but I was a former coal miner; that I had received my training as a Socialist in the ranks of the South Wales Miners' Federation and I was proud of my background, and of the men with whom I had worked and of their untiring efforts in the cause of Socialism. This first meeting passed off without any trouble but in the following meeting I was confronted with several pro-communists and fellow travellers with whom I soon clashed. After attending a few meetings I made it clear that I was not going to be pushed about by people who spend all their time in trying to undermine the work of the Labour Party. This stand of mine, quite early after taking up my appointment, was appreciated by the large majority of delegates who gave me their support. I found Cambridge very interesting in many ways, and in particular its colleges and its book shops, where I spent as much time as possible selecting the books that I wanted to read. It was a strange experience for me to go to the Students' Union and to address a meeting of the Labour Club. I met at one of the colleges one day a young man of special interest: his name was Rowland Hill, a descendant of *the* Rowland Hill of Penny Post fame. This young student came to my office very often and I enjoyed his company very much. I think I succeeded in helping him to make up his mind to join the Labour Party though he came to Cambridge from a very strong Tory background: his father was a retired Army Officer. I arranged to go along to Rowland's room in the college for tea one day but early in the afternoon he telephoned me asking if I would put off our appointment for about an hour because his father had come to see him and he thought it better for me to go along after his father had left.

Later in the afternoon he telephoned me and said his father had left and I could then visit him and have a talk over a cup of tea. On my arrival I noticed that Rowland had a number of books, pamphlets, and so on, spread over a table in such a way that no one entering that room would fail to see them and that they were publications from the Labour Party. I enquired from Rowland what his father thought about his son's interest in the Labour Party, "I can tell you," said Rowland, "my father was very surprised and told me that he was pleased to find me interested in politics," and whilst he did not agree with the Labour Party, he thought it was better for me to be interested in their kind of politics than not to be interested in any kind.

Some years later after I had returned to Wales I met Rowland at a Labour Party meeting and introduced him to the Postmaster General, Mr George Isaacs, and arranged for them to have a photograph taken together. I thought it would be very nice for the Postmaster General to be photographed along with a descendant of *the* Rowland Hill.

The Eastern Counties, where I was Organiser, included Essex, Suffolk, Norfolk, Cambridge, Ely, Rutland, Bedford and Hertford. It was a beautiful district in which to work but this was during the War and difficult to get about. Side lights only were permitted to be used on cars and this was not very helpful during night time, and during the day I had to find my way around without the aid of signposts. On more than one occasion I was in a district which had been attacked by enemy aircraft and I spent nights in places like Cromer, Great Yarmouth, Felixstowe or Southend, when bombing took place and believe me it was not very comfortable. The district, generally speaking, was very flat with rich agricultural land. I can remember travelling toward Wisbech one day, when I thought I had run into a sand storm: it was the wind blowing the dry soil to such an extent that I was forced to pull in on the side of the road because I could not see to drive my car and this was early in the afternoon. When the wind died down my car was in a filthy condition and I had to clean all the soil off the windows before I could proceed. On another occasion, I was travelling through the district making for a particular village when I stopped and asked for directions from a gentleman on the side of the road. I was a little surprised when he told me continue on the road for about a mile then I would come to a hill and in a short distance over the brow, I would see a road on my left. I was to take that road for about a mile. I must say I was very confused and as I travelled along looking for the hill I did not find it so went some miles out of my way.

The district had an industrial belt in the London part of Essex and in parts of Bedford, which included Luton. In these areas many people from Wales had settled during the industrial depression. When attending meetings in these parts it was very much like being with people from South Wales who had experienced hardship and were determined to bring about a change in society. In any case the people throughout the whole of the Eastern Counties were friendly, reliable, hard working. In those constituencies which had never been won by the Labour Party, men and women were loyal and made their own contribution on behalf of Socialism which meant so much to them.

I cannot leave the Eastern Counties without mentioning Miss Gertrude Frances who was my colleague and in charge of the women's branches of our organisation and who lived with a Miss Bamford, a school teacher, in a beautiful cottage named 'Old Thatch', situated in the village of Beyton in the county of Suffolk. These two ladies had lived in the district for some years and knew every inch of it, so from them I learned much of the geography of the Eastern Counties and, which was much more important, I gained from them much valuable information about the people and their way of life. 'Old Thatch' was, as I said, a very beautiful cottage but it was not small but big enough to provide accommodation for several people and for me it was a haven of rest. Mr George Shepherd, when he wished to see me for discussion, would arrange for our meeting to take place in

'Old Thatch' where we would, of course, spend the night. I well remember my first meeting with Mr George Shepherd during a weekend at 'Old Thatch', soon after I commenced my duties in the Eastern Counties. He turned to me at the dining table and said, "You will always find a welcome here in 'Old Thatch' Cliff and you must come as often as you wish". He then turned to the two ladies of the house and said, "I am sure you will welcome Cliff at all times." These two women had an excellent working arrangement concerning the duties of looking after the home and their guests. I established an office which was reasonably central for my district and it gave me an opportunity to meet people and talk with them in the privacy of my office, on matters relative to the Labour Party and its future. On my visits to Bedford and Hertford I would meet George Brown (later Lord George Brown) who was at that time a full-time officer of the Transport and General Workers Union. George was, also, very active in the Labour Party and an Honorary Secretary of the County Federation of the Labour Party. I always found him to be most helpful in all the meetings which I attended. Though many of my meetings were difficult and I was a stranger in strange surroundings, I could always rely upon George to come to my assistance. I mention in particular that George worked his way in the Labour Party by carrying out the very ordinary duties expected from the grass roots of our Movement and no one can ever accuse him of jumping on to the band wagon. Yes, George worked hard in the building of the Labour Party and I am glad of this opportunity to place on record my appreciation of his services. I was very happy in the Eastern Counties where I made a number of friends who were also very good Socialists. The kind of work in which I was engaged was not only interesting but it was also a new experience because so much of my time and service was concerned with the personal approach. I was anxious to make my home in Cambridge and in fact had made provisional arrangements to rent a suitable house so that my wife could come along from Glynneath and join me. However this was not to be. I received a telephone call from Labour Party Headquarters in London with the shocking news that my colleague and dear friend George Morris, Organiser of the Labour Party in Wales, had been killed in a bombing raid over Cardiff while he was carrying out his duties fire watching in Charles Street near his office. I asked the National Agent if I should go to Cardiff immediately. He agreed and said I should get away as soon as possible and not come back to Cambridge until after the funeral. I travelled to Cardiff by car and then onto Glynneath, but often wonder how I was able to drive because my heart felt so heavy and my eyes were not dry. George had been such a good Organiser but he had also been a very good friend to me and I appreciated his friendship and his many qualities. His passing away would mean so much to the Labour Party and it would indeed be difficult to find a suitable successor. I would not be an applicant because in my opinion I did not have the experience necessary and therefore the Labour Party National Executive Committee should look around its staff for a very experienced person.

In due course the job was advertised and without my asking, an application form was sent to me with a request that I should complete same and return to our Head Office at Transport House, London. I simply put the form away and had no intention of making an application. However time was going on, and the day before the final day for receipt of applications arrived without me taking any action. I received a telephone call from the National Agent of the Labour Party pointing out that my application form had not been received. I was then asked to complete the form and send it off that very day so that it would reach London on the very last day for me to comply with the advert. I was told if I did not apply, the National Executive Committee reserved the right to transfer me to Wales if they thought it necessary, and therefore it would be better for me to apply than to be posted against my wishes.

9

Return to Wales

I must confess I was not over anxious to return to Wales though I loved Wales and was proud to be a Welshman, but I had been in the Eastern Counties for such a short time and was just getting to know the people in that part of England. They were a very reserved people and took their time in getting to know a stranger in their midst, but once they got to know you they were a delightful people, very kind, very sociable and helpful in so many ways.

However I received information that I was placed on a short list of applicants to appear before the appropriate sub-committee of the National Executive Committee of the Labour Party relative to the appointment of a Regional Organiser of the Labour Party in Wales. After we were all interviewed, I was officially informed that the decision of the committee was unanimous in recommending that I was to be appointed. This was confirmed by the National Executive Committee and I returned to the land of my birth to take over the very responsible job of Organiser for the Labour Party throughout Wales and also the secretaryship of the South Wales Regional Council of Labour. Arrangements were made for the Executive Committee of the South Wales Regional Council to be called together, when I was accompanied by Mr George Shepherd, National Agent, Mr George Ridley and Mr Harold Laski, who were members of the Committee responsible for my appointment. I was presented to a body of people, all of whom I knew personally and with whom I had worked in the movement in South Wales. I was given a very warm welcome and a promise of full support on behalf of the Labour and Trade Union Movement in Wales.

I was very conscious of the fact that I was following my friend the late Mr George Morris who had been such an efficient organiser and, after all, I was such a new member of the Labour staff. But I was not a new boy to the Labour and Trade Union Movement in South Wales. I had been for many years active in the South Wales Miners' Federation and had held office at branch and district level. The political movement was not unknown to me, because I had served as voluntary secretary to the Glynneath Ward Labour Party, the Vale of Neath Trades Council and Labour Party, the Neath Constituency Labour Party and also the Glamorgan Federation of Labour Parties. Now in 1943 I became Secretary of the South Wales Regional Council of Labour and Organiser of the Labour Party in Wales. This Regional Council was unique because it was the only one of its kind in Britain, it was political and industrial. Its dual functions were recognised by both the National Executive Committee of the Labour Party and the General Council of the Trades Union Congress. It was given birth in 1937 in the midst of much trouble in the political and industrial movement in South Wales. The Communists were very active in the Trade Union Movement, and its agents and fellow travellers were working underneath a cloak in a number of our local Labour Parties. A Council of Action was about to be set up in Cardiff, which would have been made up of representatives of trade unions and the Labour Parties who were not in full support of the Labour Party. This move was handicapped by the foresight of Mr George Morris who advised the General Council of the TUC and the NEC of the Labour Party to permit him to form the Regional Council and this was agreed by both national organisations and they helped to finance the new organisation until it got over its teething troubles. It was fortunate for me that I had been consulted concerning the need for its formation and I took part in the drafting of its rules and standing orders. It was also in our favour that the Regional Council was housed in Transport House, in Charles Street, Cardiff, which was also the offices of the Transport and General Workers Union whose General Secretary was Mr Ernest Bevin, a good supporter of the Regional Council.

During the war years, there was a political truce· which meant that if a parliamentary seat became vacant the main political parties would not contest the election but the party which held the seat prior to the vacancy would appoint a new Member of Parliament. This, of course, did not always work smoothly because it gave rise to splinter groups and there was no shortage of them. Furthermore, this truce had many disadvantages because it left constituency and local Labour Parties without any real work to do because there was no incentive. It is well known that a political party without any real activities in its own field will soon die for the want of doing those things that keep party politics alive. Not only was there a truce for parliamentary elections but it also applied to local government elections. This, of course, had a disastrous effect on party morale and on the Labour Party membership in particular, especially in the industrial districts where electioneering had been the life-blood of the Labour Party. It was, therefore, necessary for me to spend much of my time in travelling throughout the Principality making personal contacts in order to keep members together in the interest of future activities. A number of our local parties in rural districts were placed in cold storage because, apart from having less work to do, their officers were away engaged in war service.

On a regional basis we found plenty of activity through the work of sub-committees that had been given special responsibility to prepare memoranda on the kind of things we would like to have established once the war was over. At that particular time the Regional Council spent much time in discussing such questions as Home Rule for Wales, or the appointment of a Secretary of State for the Principality. The subject of Home Rule was most certainly turned down by the great majority of our movement but the question of having a Secretary of State found some favour as a result of much propaganda by the then Mr Ewan Morgan of Cardiganshire. In fact, the Annual Conference of the Regional Council of Labour had, in 1942, unanimously accepted the following resolution which had been submitted by the Cardiff Borough Labour Party: "That this Conference is of the opinion that the time is now opportune to press for the appointment of a Secretary of State for Wales." The 1944 Regional Conference passed a stronger resolution by demanding the appointment.

As we were drawing near to 1945, it was necessary for us to make arrangements in readiness for a General Election. The position in Wales was that out of thirty six seats in Parliament, nineteen were held by Labour Party members and eighteen of these were in South Wales.

It is also worthy to note that no less than thirteen of the Members of Parliament in South Wales were members of the South Wales Miners' Federation and were sponsored by the said Union. They were political giants in the Labour and Trade Union Movement and I place on record their names and the constituencies they represented: Messrs James Griffiths, Llanelli; D. R. Grenfell, Gower; William Jenkins, Neath; Ted Williams, Ogmore; William John, Rhondda West; W. H. Mainwaring, Rhondda East; S. O. Davies, Merthyr; George Hall, Aberdare; Ness Edwards, Caerphilly; Charles Edwards, Bedwellty; Aneurin Bevan, Ebbw Vale; George Dagger, Abertillery, and Arthur Jenkins, Pontypool.

It will be noted that the Members of Parliament sponsored by the South Wales Miners' Federation held their seats in the industrial belt of South Wales, where coal was mined. I personally regret very much that there is not now one Member of Parliament in Wales sponsored by the South Wales Miners' Federation. The last two were S. O. Davies, Merthyr, and Elved Davies, Rhondda East.

The War with Germany came to an end in 1945 and political parties got down to prepare for the General Election. I can assure you that there was no shortage of prospective candidates and the General Election provided an opportunity for those who wished to embark on a political career, though it must be said in all fairness that not many careerists succeeded on jumping onto the band waggon in Wales though it was not for the want of trying. Prior to the Election, we organised in Wales a number of weekend and day schools for the purpose of discussing and coming to an agreement on such questions as procedure for nomination and selection of candidates, and this was very necessary because there were so many of our party officers not accustomed to the selection of candidates. We also discussed tactics and the way to make full use of Members of Parliament in safe seats in the work for and on behalf of the candidates in the other constituencies. We were anxious to break through if possible in North Wales, where at that time we held only one seat, that of Wrexham, held by Mr Robert Richards. To have any success in North Wales meant that attention had to be paid to the Welsh language, especially on the kind of literature and posters we would display. Off I went to Bangor and met Mr David Thomas who was a life long Socialist, an ardent Welshman and a scholar, who had never lost the common touch. I invited him to draft a number of attractive posters in the Welsh language. He readily accepted my invitation and prepared some of the most attractive posters ever published by the Labour Party. We had also to consider the cultural side of our policy and it was natural for me to go to David Thomas for he was the very man to prepare the right kind of material to appeal to the electors in North Wales, Our candidates in North Wales were themselves very concerned with the Welsh language and with other issues on behalf of Wales. This led one or two of them in the north western corner of the

Principality to publish an Election Broadsheet under the title of *Llais Llafur* which was the name of a newspaper favouring the Labour Party and published in the Swansea Valley. The meaning of *Llais Llafur* is 'Labour's Voice.' I must emphasise that it was not a Labour Party newspaper, though generally speaking it supported our policy. In the Broadhseet published, our people got a little too enthusiastic and promised some form of Home Rule for Wales. And for some years after the Welsh Nationalists would refer to that publication claiming that the Labour Party in Wales had in 1945 promised Home Rules for Wales and I spent much of my time in pointing out that the Broadsheet was not on behalf of the Labour Party but was published by a few people in North West Wales without the authority of the Labour Party.

Well, we entered the campaign and there was a demand from all constituencies for speakers to explain our policy to the electors. The allocation of speakers was a part of my job and I had to take great care in making the proper use of the limited number of speakers available. I then took the view, and continue to hold it, that for a speaker to be of any advantage, he or she should be selected with care to suit the area in which the speaker was required. This was and still is of vital importance in certain parts of the Principality. This meant that there were some speakers suggested by Transport House, London, which I had to reluctantly refuse to accept in the interest of a good campaign. That was not altogether a popular decision but I was simply concerned with the giving of good service and the winning of the General Election.

Finance plays an important part in the kind of organisation that can be placed in the field in support of candidates and our policy. The constituencies with candidates sponsored by Trade Unions had no need to worry unduly over money to pay for the campaign, but about half of our candidates had no financial backing. I, therefore, established a central fund for the whole of Wales in order to help those candidates who had no financial support of any kind. The South Wales miners made a very handsome donation to the fund so that the constituencies in need of money could be helped. It should in fairness be recorded that the South Wales Miners' Federation always came to the aid of the non-industrial constituencies who had little or no finance. The constituency parties were very independent and would have no talk about finance when selecting a parliamentary candidate. Indeed they would make it clear that money did not count but would concentrate on selecting what they considered to be the best candidate for their area. However, immediately they had selected their candidate, they would enquire about financial support and in the absence of any, they would make an appeal for help from the Central Fund. This was fair enough but it was strange how some constituencies with trade union sponsored candidates would come along asking for money from the Central Fund. However, it was a strict rule that the funds should be used to assist those constituencies which had no financial support; they were to be helped and no others. There was also a National Fund organised by the Labour Party set up for the purpose of helping those constituencies in need.

As you can imagine, the campaign brought a number of journalists into my office who were concerned with the way things were likely to go. Those who came from abroad were particularly interested in Rhondda East where our candidate was Mr W. H. Mainwaring who was opposed by Mr Harry Pollitt, one of the leading Communists in Britain at that time. It was very interesting to find that the journalists from abroad gave a clear impression that they expected Mr Pollitt to win the seat. The Communist Party put everything possible into the fight in that constituency and we in turn left nothing to chance. The most frustrating part of that General Election was the long wait before the result was known and this arose from the fact that for that particular election, members of HM Forces serving abroad were allowed to vote. This meant a delay of three weeks before all the ballot papers could be brought together and counted. A day was fixed for counting to take place throughout the whole country and the results would then be made known the same day.

I waited patiently for that date and had prepared in my office a large chart with all the constituencies in Wales and their candidates shown boldly so that places were reserved for the result of the voting in the constituencies could be recorded and easily seen. I wanted to keep a look out for the results in certain marginal constituencies and at the same time I could disregard any information that would be coming over the telephone from the industrial belt, where the constituencies were safe for the Labour candidates.

The great day arrived. Before noon, we had one or two results coming in over the telephone and then throughout the afternoon we had the great bulk of reports available. My chart revealed that we were gaining seats in Wales and this gave me great delight and it would also give great pleasure to the many voluntary workers who had worked so hard in all parts of Wales during the campaign. As we entered the results on our chart we also kept in touch with our Head Office in London and they were able to give me, from time to time, a clear picture of what was happening throughout the country.

About mid-afternoon, when most of the results were known, I received a call from Mr Len Hill, our Election Agent for Mr George Dagger in the Abertillery Constituency. I, of course, had already marked my chart with a sure win for this constituency because it was looked upon as a very safe Labour seat. However, over the telephone Len Hill started to apologise for being so late in giving the result and went on to explain that there had been a re-count. This shook me and I blurted out, "What on earth went wrong in this safe seat for you to have a re-count?" Len replied. "Well, the Tory candidate just saved his deposit by a couple of hundred votes so we demanded a re-count to see if we could make him lose his deposit. That is why we are late, but we failed to make him lose his deposit." I gave a sigh of relief but have on many occasions had a good laugh over that incident and indeed I could never understand why the Returning Officer granted a re-count. It also occurred to me that our people were not satisfied with inflicting a heavy defeat on the Tory candidate, they wanted to rub salt in the wound. The result of the poll in Abertillery was Mr George Dagger 28,615 and to the Tory candidate 4,422: it will be seen that the latter saved his deposit by less than two hundred votes. This is a very good story and perhaps it explains in some way the feelings at that time between supporters of the Labour Party and those of the Tory Party.

That day of the counting and the re-counting of the votes was most certainly a very memorable day in the history of the Labour Party and the feelings of lots of people were expressed to me at the end of that day when all results were known. Councillor A. J. Williams, one of the senior members of Cardiff City Council, came to my office and took me by the hand and said, "Cliff, I feel like throwing my cap up into the air because we have at last achieved something for which I have worked all my life." How right he was in his expression on behalf of his generation, for they had not only sown the seeds on behalf of the Labour Party, but had put in every effort in order to achieve success. In the following pages I give the result of the General Election in every constituency in Wales from which it will be noted that the workers on behalf of the Labour Party had gained seven seats and lost just one in Carmarthen, because the sitting member of Parliament Mr R. Moelwyn Hughes was a patient at Sully Hospital throughout the whole of the campaign.

GENERAL ELECTION RESULTS IN WALES, 1945

Angelsey

Lloyd-George, Lady Megan.	(Lib)	12,610
Hughes, Flg Officer. C	(Lab)	11,529
	Lib Maj.	1,081

Brecon & Radnor

Watkins, T. E.	(Lab)	19,725
Guest, Maj. O.	(Con)	14,089
Lewis, D. L.	(Lib)	8,335
	Lab Maj.	5,636

Caernarfon

Roberts, G. O.	(Lab)	22,043
Owen, Sir G.	(Lib)	15,637
Bebb, W. A.	(Welsh Nat)	2,152
	Lab Maj.	6,406
	Lab Gain.	

Cardigan

Bowen, Capt. R.	(Lib)	18,192
Morgan, Iwan.	(Lab)	10,718
	Lib Maj.	8,194

Carmarthen

Morris, R. H.	(Lib)	19,783
Hughes, R. M.	(Lab)	18,504
	Lib Maj.	1.279
	Lib Gain.	

Llanelly

Griffiths, J.	(Lab)	44,514
George, Maj. G. O.	(Con)	10,397
	Lab Maj.	34,117

1.   The author in H.M. Forces, 1918.

2. Carnival in Glynneath during the 1921 coal miners' strike.

3.   Peeling potatoes outside the soup kitchen at Glynneath during the 1921 coal miners' strike.

4. Cutting coal at a small mine for the fires of the soup kitchens during the strike of 1926.

5. Part of the Committee responsible for running the soup kitchens, 1926,
The author is pictured holding a basket of loaves.

6. Cliff and Vi, 1932.

8.	With George Morris at a Labour Party conference, 1939.

7.	A group of workers near the colliery screen at Glynneath, September, 1935.

9.   Opening a child welfare clinic at Glynneath, 1939.

10. The Welsh delegates at the Labour Party conference in Southport, 1939.

12. Rowland Hill, descendant of the 'Penny Post' Rowland Hill, with Cliff Prothero, 1943.

11. The author, 1942.

13. Jack Richards; Granville West, Labour candidate; the author; and Morgan Phillips, General Secretary of the Labour Party, at the Pontypool by-election, 1946.

14. The Executive Committee of the Welsh Council of Labour, 1948. Members pictured include George Thomas, M.P.; Goronwy Roberts, M.P.; Mrs. D.T. Jenkins, Chairman.

15. The Rt. Hon. Herbert Morrison, M.P., at a memorial service to Robert Owen in the churchyard at Newtown, 1949.

16. The Rt. Hon. C.R. Attlee, Prime Minister, in Llandudno, September, 1949, pictured with Alderman H.T. Edwards, Owen Edwards and the author.

17. Lady Megan Lloyd George after the election victory in Carmarthen, March 1, 1957, with Islwyn Thomas and the author.

18. A small group including U Thant, Secretary General of the United Nations, 1958.

19.   The Rt. Hon. Hugh Gaitskell, M.P., and Mrs. Gaitskell arriving at Cardiff, 1961.

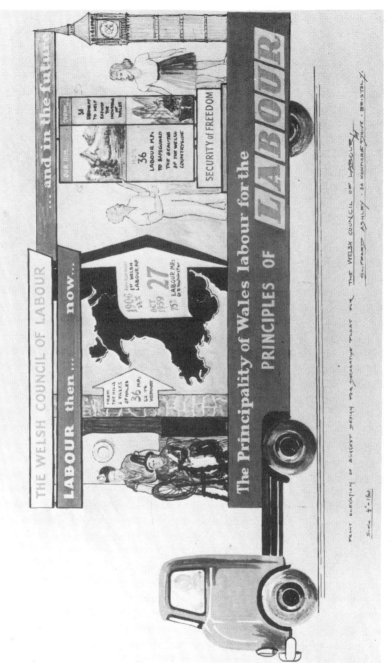

20. The Welsh Council of Labour float designed for the Festival of Labour in London, 1962.

21. The Rt. Hon. Harold Wilson, M.P., opening the General Election campaign in Cardiff, September, 26, 1964.

22. Cliff Prothero at his desk, February, 1981.

Denbigh

Morris-Jones, Sir H.	(Lib Nat)	17,023
Evans, Wg-Cdr. G.	(Lib)	12,101
Jones, Lt-Cdr. W. L. M.	(Lab)	11,702
	Lib Nat Maj.	4,922

Wrexham

Richards, R.	(Lab)	26,854
Miln, D. L.	(Nat)	13,714
Williams, J. D.	(Lib)	6,960
Jones, J. R. H.	(Welsh Nat)	430
	Lab Maj.	13,140

Flint

Birch, Lt-Col. N.	(Con)	27,800
Jones, Miss E. L.	(Lab)	26,761
Hughes, J. W.	(Lib)	17,007
	Con Maj.	1,039

Aberavon

Cove, W. G.	(Lab)	31,286
Llewellyn, Capt. D. T.	(Con)	11,860
	Lab Maj.	19.426

Caerphilly

Edwards, Ness.	(Lab)	29,158
de Courcy, Capt. J.	(Con)	7,189
	Lab Maj.	21,969

Gower

Grenfell, D. R.	(Lab)	30,676
Aeron-Thomas, J.	(Lib Nat)	14,115
	Lab Maj.	16,561

Llandaff & Barry

Ungoed-Thomas, Maj. L.	(Lab)	33,706
Lakin, C.	(Con)	27,108
Williams, Maj. B.	(Lib)	10,132
	Lab Maj.	6,958
	Lab Gain.	

Neath

Williams, D. J.	(Lab)	37,957
Bowen, D. J.	(Nat)	8,466
Samuel, W.	(Welsh Nat)	3,659
	Lab Maj.	29,491

Ogmore

Williams, E. J.	(Lab)	32,715
Davies, Maj. O. G.	(Nat)	7,712
Morgan, T.	(Welsh Nat)	2,379
	Lab Maj.	25,003

Pontypridd

Pearson, A.	(Lab)	27,823
Treherne, Capt. C. G.	(Con)	7,260
Williams, J. E.	(Lib)	5,464
	Lab Maj.	20,563

Merioneth

Roberts, Sgn. Ldr. E. C.	(Lib)	8,496
Jones, H. M.	(Lab)	8,383
Hughes, C. P.	(Con)	4,374
Evans, G.	(Welsh Nat)	2,448
	Lib Maj.	112

Abertillery

Dagger, G.	(Lab)	28,615
Hayward, Surg. Cmdr. J. J.	(Nat)	4,422
	Lab Maj.	24,193

Bedwellty

Edwards, Sir C.	(Lab)	30,480
Tett, Lt. H. I.	(Con)	6,641
	Lab Maj.	23,839

Ebbw Vale

Bevan, A.	(Lab)	27,209
Parker, Flt. Lt. S. C.	(Con)	6,758
	Lab Maj.	20.451

Monmouth

Pym, L. R.	(Con)	22,195
Oakley, A. L.	(Lab)	20,543
	Con Maj.	1,652

Pontypool

Jenkins, A.	(Lab)	27,455
Weeple, J. G.	(Con)	8,072
	Lab Maj.	19,383

Montgomery

Davies, Clement	(Lib)	14,018
Owen, Capt. P. L. W.	(Con)	10,895
	Lib Maj.	3,123

Pembroke

Lloyd-George, Maj. G.	(Lib)	22,997
Fienburgh, Maj. W.	(Lab)	22,829
	Lib Maj.	168

Cardiff Central

Thomas, T. G.	(Lab)	16,506
Hallinan, C. S.	(Con)	11,982
Morgan, Lt. P. H.	(Lib)	5,121
	Lab Maj.	4,524
	Lab Gain.	

Cardiff East

Marquand, Prof. H. A.	(Lab)	16,299
Grigg, Sir. J.	(Nat)	11,306
Emlyn-Jones, J. E.	(Lib)	4,523
	Lab Maj.	4,993
	Lab Gain.	

Cardiff South

Callaghan, Lt. L. J. A.	(Lab)	17,489
Evans, Sir A.	(Con)	11,545
	Lab Maj.	4,944
	Lab Gain.	

Caernarfon Boroughs

White, Lt. Col. D. Price	(Con)	11,432
Davies, D. S.	(Lib)	11,096
Jones, W. E.	(Lab)	10,625
	Con Maj.	336
	Con Gain from Lib	

Merthyr Tydfil

Davies, S. O.	(Lab)	24,879
Jennings, S.	(Ind)	5,693
	Lab Maj.	19,186

Aberdare

Hall, George.	(Lab)	34,398
Clover, Capt. C. G.	(Con)	6,429
	Lab Maj.	27,969

Newport

Freeman, P.	(Lab)	23,845
Bell, Lt-Comdr. R. M.	(Con)	14,754
Crawsnay, Maj. W. R.	(Lib)	5,362
	Lab Maj.	9,091
	Lab Gain.	

Rhondda East

Mainwaring, W. H.	(Lab)	16,733
Pollitt, H.	(Comm)	15,761
Davies, J.K.	(Welsh Nat)	2,123
	Lab Maj.	972

Rhondda West

John, W.	Unopposed Lab.

Swansea East

Mort, D. L.	(Lab)	18,127
Harding, R.	(Lib Nat)	6,102
	Lab Maj.	12,025

Swansea West

Morris, P.	(Lab)	18,098
Jones, Sir L.	(Lib Nat)	13,089
	Lab Maj.	5,099
	Lab Gain.	

Universities:
Wales

Gruffydd, Prof. W. J.	(Lib)	5,239
Jones, Miss G.	(Welsh Nat)	1,696

I record for future reference that there were 36 parliamentary constituencies, including the University, and the result of this General Election was Labour 25 seats, Liberal 7 seats, Liberal National 1 seat and the Conservatives 3 seats.

Our supporters up and down the country rejoiced, which was understandable but it was also a time of great responsibility and our movement had to change its attitude from one of opposition to that of Government in charge of the affairs of the nation. The Regional Council of Labour had for some time been submitting memoranda on such questions as Economy, Agriculture, Employment and Devolution. It now, following such a victory, took a little time to consider what changes were required in its own organisation and came to the conclusion that there should be one voice on behalf of the Labour and trade union movement for the whole of Wales. It was true then, as now, that a great part of the population resides in the southern parts of the Principality. But there were trade unions in North Wales and also nine constituency Labour Parties with hardly any voice in the decision making of the Regional Council of Labour. It is true that a Federation of Constituency Labour Parties functioned in North Wales and from time to time expressed itself on behalf of North Wales but some of us felt that it should be brought into the main stream of political activities for and on behalf of the Principality. Proposals were therefore considered with a view to extending the Regional Council of Labour so that it would cover and speak for the whole of Wales. I took the opportunity of discussing this matter with the National Agent of the Labour Party who was very sympathetic but thought it could not be arranged because of geographical difficulties and the great distance between, for instance, Angelsey and Cardiff. I was already covering the whole of Wales as Organiser of the Labour Party and this created an anomaly which I was determined to remove in the interest of the Principality and of our movement. In North Wales there was already a Federation of Labour Parties where the matter could be fully discussed. In all our discussions we had to seriously consider ways and means of giving North Wales representation on the Executive Committee and how to be able to pay the expenses of members travelling down to Cardiff because the party in North Wales could not be expected to face such costs. During further discussions with the National Agent I asked for financial assistance for the specific purpose of paying travelling expenses to North Wales representatives only. My request was taken to the National Executive Committee of the Labour Party and it was agreed that a grant of £100 per annum for a couple of years should be made. Agreement was reached between the South Wales Regional Council and the North Wales Federation of Labour Parties that there shall be one organisation for the Labour Party and trade union movement for the whole of the Principality. This was confirmed by all concerned including the Trades Union Congress. There were difficulties to be overcome because the Labour Parties and trade unions were much stronger in South Wales than in North Wales and there was a danger that members of the Executive Committee, who were elected by ballot, would all come from South Wales. To avoid this we reserved a couple of seats for representatives from North Wales Labour parties and a couple for the North Wales trade unions.

I was very pleased with the support and co-operation received from all concerned in the introduction of this new kind of organisation for the whole of Wales. There was however another one thing to be done in our endeavour to speak for the whole of the Labour and trade union movement in the Principality. It was obvious that our title could no longer be Regional Council so the proposal was put forward that we should now be called the Council of

Labour for Wales. Some slight opposition to this was envisaged, but we secured the help of such influential leaders as Jim Griffiths and Herbert Morrison, who were most helpful and assured us of success. So our new title was agreed which meant a step forward. The Council of Labour could speak with one voice and put forward proposals in a much clearer way than the movement had been able to do in the past. Following these arrangements an article appeared in the *Labour Organiser,* July 14th 1947, written by one known as 'Jack Cutter' in the following terms:

PROFILE BY JACK CUTTER   No. 11 CLIFF PROTHERO

THE VOICE OF WALES

At every one of the forty-odd Labour Party Annual Conferences up to and including Margate, 1947, there has been a very vocal, determined and eloquent minority whose views are shared by a relatively small section of the Party membership. But they argue their case with such force and persuasiveness and with such a steady stream of speakers succeeding each other at the rostrum, amid storms of applause from their supporters in the visitors' gallery, that the non-supporting visitor could be excused for thinking in consternation that the Conference was allowing the majority case to go by default.

I recall one such occasion about ten Conferences ago when the Party was being urged to join one of the several "fronts" which annually cluttered up our agendas in the immediate pre-war years. This time the pro-fronters were more than usually vociferous and numerous, a queue of prophets of doom lining up at the rostrum to reiterate each other's case with such monotony that the attention wandered. Yet another speaker started and I had begun to consider whether there was time to slip out to the tea room and back before the vote was taken when my attention was arrested by the new speaker's manner and matter.

Forthright Clarity

Here was someone putting the other point of view at last, and putting it with forthright clarity. Conference was literally sitting up and taking notice. Soon the "hear, hears" were greeting every sentence with growing volume. The clear, emphatic voice went on saying bluntly to Conference what we all knew the mass of the membership had been saying in the Party meetings throughout the country.

I turned to my neighbour, who was that fine colleague, the late George Morris, D. O. for Wales. "This is one of your boys," I said, "Who is he?" "His name is Cliff Prothero." said George, "He is Chairman of Neath D.I.P. and a coming lad. You will be hearing more of him."

Although Cliff made his reputation in the wider movement by that speech he was already well known throughout South Wales. At 15 he joined the South Wales Miners' Federation and at 21 he was vice-chairman of a lodge of over 1,000 members at Glynneath in Glamorgan. Throughout his twenties he was in every phase of the South Wales Miners' struggle.

In 1936 he went to the U.S.S.R. as one of the miners' delegation, and throughout all these years he played his active part in the political side of the movement as an officer of his D.I.P. and as a Labour member of that important local authority known as the Neath Rural District Council, although it serves a huge urban population, larger than many a fully-fledged borough.

Back to Wales

In 1942, when Morgan Phillips, then D.O. for the Eastern Counties, became Research Officer of the Party, Cliff was appointed to his place, but his time in East Anglia was cut short by a tragic circumstance. George Morris was killed by enemy action in an air-raid while on fire-watching duty near his Cardiff office.

We read of this news with the numbing shock of stunned dismay, for George was an efficient, popular and indeed beloved colleague and friend. Yet, in the midst of the feelings of desolation, the thought must have occurred to many as it did to me: "Cliff will go back to Wales now." And he did. It seemed the obvious thing to do.

The news of his new appointment was, somehow, cheering and reassuring. Cliff had always seemed to me so dependable, solid, reliable. Good old clear-cut, forthright Cliff, always poised and never posing. He would be all right.

It is ten years since the South Wales Regional Council of Labour was formed. This year it becomes the Welsh Regional Council of Labour covering the whole of Wales. It is the only Regional Council with Industrial and Political Sections. There are historical reasons for this with their roots in the stormy days of the early thirties when conflicting interests and policies were backing at the foundations of the Welsh movement.

Welsh Unity

It was a master stroke to create a single, unifying organisation to which all who believed in practical unity could rally politically and industrially, and against the solidity of which all the lip-serving "miners" could batter in vain, exposed as a stage army, marching off left and whizzing round the backcloth to reappear breathlessly right.

Under Cliff Prothero's guidance the Regional Council has trebled its territory, extended its scope and influence and consolidated its already strong position. Cliff would be the last person to claim any credit for this, for he has always regarded it as a natural development which was bound to come, but he saw that it did come, smoothly and without fuss or upheaval in the manner that indicates that good, solid groundwork has been well and carefully done.

And those last four words very aptly sum up everything that Cliff sets his hand to do.

10

The Council for Wales

The Council now representing the whole of Wales considered very seriously the kind of proposals to submit on behalf of the Principality in the field of devolution. At two previous Annual Meetings it had been decided to demand that the Government should appoint a Secretary of State for Wales. Members of the Executive Committee had been invited to submit memoranda on the kind of devolution required and at the Annual Meeting in 1948 the Executive Committee presented the following report which was accepted:

> During the course of the year, the Executive Committee had under active consideration the need for affording Wales a greater measure of self-determination. It reached the conclusion that the proposal for the appointment of a Secretary of State for Wales was no longer practicable, and could not be fruitfully pursued and, therefore, prepared an alternative policy of a more comprehensive nature, based on 'Democratic Devolution' which was discussed with a view to its implementation by the Government. Quite an amount of memoranda were prepared and submitted to the Executive Committee for consideration and then in turn to the Welsh Parliamentary Labour Group for joint discussion. The Group then prepared its own document outlining its case and after a good deal of discussion, agreement was reached on a Joint Memorandum. There was however a strong minority within the Welsh Parliamentary Labour Group very much against the proposals for devolution.

The Annual Meeting in 1948 also resolved:

> That this Annual Meeting of the Welsh Council of Labour, having received a report of the proposals to urge H.M. Government to establish an Advisory Council for Wales composed of representatives of Welsh life, for the purpose of advising the Government and its Agents on the need for appropriate legislation to meet the requirements of Wales from time to time.

It was further resolved to give full power to the Executive Committee to continue its negotiations with representatives of HM Government with the view of getting the proposals implemented. Arrangements were made for H.M. Government to receive the following deputation: Messrs W. G. Cove, MP; George Dagger, MP; D. J. Williams, MP; Arthur Pearson, MP; and Goronwy Roberts, MP, representing the Labour Group, and Messrs C.W. Bridges, Lewis Lewis, Gwyn Thomas, H. T. Edwards, Mrs D. T. Jenkins and Cliff Prothero representing the Regional Council of Labour. The Joint Memorandum was fully discussed with representatives of H M Government when a fair amount of agreement was reached. It was necessary to have more than one meeting and in the meantime there was much off-the-record discussion. I had, of course, from time to time discussed the matter very fully with Mr Jim Griffiths who was a member of the Government and also a member of the National Executive Committee of the Labour Party. It was also very fortunate for us in Wales that Mr Herbert Morrison was in charge of our negotiations on behalf of the Government. He was a very valued friend of mine and I was able to meet him on several occasions in his room in the House of Commons for the purpose of discussing our proposals. The Government, having received the views of the Labour Movement in Wales, prepared its own memorandum which was very fully discussed at our joint meetings. In fact the Government proposals did not differ a great deal from our own so it was not difficult to reach agreement. The Regional Council of Labour was kept fully informed and approved the action taken by its representatives. The whole scheme as approved by the joint deputation and the Government was then submitted to the Annual Meeting of the Labour Party in Wales in May 1948, when it received full support.

We, therefore, went forward and agreed what was called 'The Government's 27-Member Council for Wales Plan.' Its terms of reference were as follows:

1 To meet from time to time and at least quarterly, for the interchange of views and information on the development and trends in economic and the cultural field in Wales and Monmouthshire.

2 To ensure that the Government is adequately informed of the impact of Government activities on the general life of the people of Wales and Monmouthshire.

Composition

Local Authorities	12
Industry including Agriculture	4
Trade Unions	4
National Eisteddfod	1
Joint Education Committee	1
University of Wales	1
Welsh Tourist Board	1
Prime Minister's Appointment	3
Total	**27**

Following the announcement of the Government's plan for Wales, it was resolved that this Executive Committee representing the Labour and trade union movement in Wales, unanimously welcome the Government's proposal and congratulate the Government upon its proposal to give Wales more than any other Government has ever offered.

I had further discussion with Mr Herbert Morrison who was very anxious that I should be one of the Prime Minster's appointments to the Council. I declined the invitation and suggested that I could be of greater service to the people of Wales by not accepting membership of this proposed Council. Mr Morrison accepted my point of view and we then went on to discuss the chairmanship, which we both considered to be of very great importance. I suggested the name of Mr. H. T. Edwards and was advised that the same name had been put forward by Mr Jim Griffiths and our advice was accepted: Mr H. T. Edwards was appointed.

A great deal of thought was behind the formation of the Council for Wales and if we look again at its composition it will be seen that every aspect of Welsh life had been covered. Some of us had from the very outset been in favour of making it something more than an economic council because we considered that the cultural way of life was of tremendous importance and therefore this was reflected in the membership of the Council. The Council when established cancelled out the demand for the appointment of a Secretary of State for Wales.

I am glad to make it known how very grateful I was to Mr George Viner, who was at that time a journalist working in South Wales for the *Daily Herald*, who gave me valuable assistance in the preparation of memoranda for submission to the Welsh Labour Group of Members of Parliament.

The Council started off well and produced some very valuable reports but it was somewhat handicapped because it had only a part-time Secretary who was seconded from one of the Government Departments. I took it upon myself to meet Mr H. T. Edwards, the Chairman, and Sir William Jones, an influential member of the Council representing the Local Authorities and suggested to them that, "In order to have a successful Council they should secure agreement that the Council put forward a request for its own full-time Secretary with a staff for the purpose of conducting research." This I considered to be of vital importance to enable the Council to function effectively in the interest of the people of Wales. Unfortunately my suggestions were not acted upon and this I considered to be one of the failures of the Council because it was not free to pursue its own policy in the preparation of the right kind of memoranda.

It is worth mentioning here that as time went on the Council continued to prepare reports which were very useful to the Labour Government but in the year 1955 another Tory Government came into power and it was obvious that the Council for Wales was an embarrassment because its reports were not in the interest of the Tory Government. The then Minister of State for Wales and Home Secretary was the Rt. Hon. H. Brooke who went along to a meeting of the Council and advised a change in the composition of the Council Membership by doing away with the representatives of the cultural organisations and handing more appointments over to the Prime Minister. This would mean that such organisations as the Welsh Joint Education Committee, the National Eisteddfod Council, the University of Wales, and the Welsh Tourist Board would no longer have the right to nominate representatives for the Council and the Prime Minister would have seven appointments instead of three. It should also be pointed out that the Prime Minister would actually make all the appointments from nominations received. For example, take the large number of Local Authorities in Wales, all permitted to nominate but not to appoint. It will there-fore be seen that the purpose of making a change in the composition was to make sure that it would be representative of the Tory Government and in so doing the cultural organisations were to be denied representation. Unfortunately the members of the Council were influenced by the Minister and accepted his proposal. That indeed was a severe blow to the very foundation of the Council and a great responsibility rested upon the shoulders of the members who were not prepared to stand up and be counted. From that day the Council lost the respect of the people of the Principality and the very purpose of the Council was destroyed.

A little later Mr H. T. Edwards resigned from the Chairmanship but it was not on the particular question mentioned above. The Welsh Nationalists with some support from within the Labour Party were campaigning for a Parliament for Wales and what had happened in the Council provided for them a platform. The Welsh Regional Council of Labour received resolutions in favour of a Parliament for Wales which were always rejected. The Labour Movement throughout Wales remained firm in its belief that a Parliament would not solve any of our problems. Though it is fair to state that a few of our Members of Parliament were sincerely in favour of a Parliament and this led to much speculation in the Press and on Radio which gave the impression that there was a rift between some Members of Parliament and the Labour Party. This was not so because it was made clear to all concerned that members of the Labour Party were free at all times to express their personal views even when at variance with Party policy. I was indeed criticised and vilified by the Welsh Nationalists because of my stand in favour of the policy laid down by the Labour Party in Wales. This did not worry me because I loved my country, Wales, and always did what I considered to be in the interest of the people of this small but important nation.

Parliament for Wales campaign

The Welsh Nationalist Party in their campaign for a separate Parliament for Wales called a convention at Llandrindod Wells on the 1st July 1950, about which I had received much information and decided to submit the following report to the Annual Meetings of the Regional Council of Labour:

> The Liberals, the Welsh Nationalists, the Welsh Republicans, and the Communists had during the General Election expressed themselves in favour of a Parliament for Wales. We are now informed an organisation calling itself the New Wales Union is convening a Convention to be held at Llandrindod Wells on the 1st July 1950 the same day as our All Wales Rally would be held in Newtown. We had received no official invitation but it had been reported in the Press that invitations would be sent to all political parties. I therefore felt that our Annual Meeting should give a lead to the Labour Movement throughout Wales on the actions which should be taken in the event of invitations being received.

The Annual Meeting therefore passed the following resolution:

> That this Regional Council of Labour dissociates itself from the Convention and calls upon the whole Labour Movement in Wales not to appoint representatives to the Convention and further that any kind of devolution required in Wales can be discussed within the confines of the Labour movement.

The report of the Secretary and the resolution mentioned above were unanimously accepted.

The Llandrindod Convention was really a flop but will be referred to in a later chapter and particularly the way it was given publicity and the methods used in order to represent the Welsh Nationalist Party to the people of Wales.

68

During this time, we in the Labour Party were concerned in not only representing the people of Wales but also in explaining to the people the benefits of having a Labour Government. We were convinced that the people appreciated what had been achieved for them since 1945 and what was still being carried out on their behalf.

11

The General Elections of 1950 and 1951

The Labour Party in Wales could have expected with some justification that the electors would give support to Labour candidates in appreciation of the work carried out by the Labour Government in face of tremendous difficulties. The coal mining industry, the electricity and gas undertakings, transport, and other services had been nationalised and great strides forward had been made in the sphere of National Insurance, Health and Social Services. In the industrial field much diversification had been brought about and many new factories had been built and were employing a large number of men and women. There had in fact over the past five years been a bloodless revolution which brought benefit to the Principality. But with all these and other successes there was something wrong within the ranks of the Labour Party and it failed to give to the public the appearance of an united party determined to continue with its purpose to bring about Socialism.

Mr Aneurin Bevan who was at that time a member of the Government had attracted a number of individuals who formed themselves into a group which was known as the Bevanites. These were in the main men and women who were disgruntled and not prepared to accept the process of democracy within the Labour Movement. It was at that time very interesting to observe how the group worked during the 1950 General Election and the following years.

There was always a shortage of speakers during any election campaign and to add to our difficulties, members of this group would only speak in constituencies where the candidate was known to be a supporter. This was very unfair because Election Agents would endeavour to get as many speakers as possible from Transport House and at the same time secure speakers from the Bevanites. This meant they were getting an increased allocation over and above what was received in the other constituencies.

I always contended and still contend that the trouble was not with Mr Aneurin Bevan but with the hangers on in the Group who made trouble for the Labour Party. The Tories took advantage of the split in our ranks and exploited it at every opportunity. I was determined to prepare our organisation in Wales to fight for Socialism and to keep in mind that our common enemy was the Tory Party. Leading up to the General Election our opponents spent great sums of money on publicity and in this respect we could not compete with them because of the cost involved. Our efforts had of necessity to be in other directions such as briefing our canvassers and making sure to have our maximum strength active in the key constituencies. We were determined to pull out all our supporters on Polling Day. Throughout Britain the Tories almost succeeded and the Labour Party suffered badly apart from here in Wales where the electors are in the main non-conformists and do not of necessity follow other parts of

Britain. I well remember listening to the results coming over the radio and the many shocks received through the loss of many seats and of very good Socialists. I kept Transport House, London, informed of the position in Wales and at the end of the day I told Mr Dick Windle, the National Agent, "I have now given to you all that we can possibly win, we have gained three seats in the constituencies of East Flint, Conway and Pembroke but we lost one in Cardiff." This meant a nett gain of two seats in Wales bringing our total number of Labour Members of Parliament up to twenty seven out of a possible thirty six. It is worthy to note that we, after that Election, had two more Labour Members of Parliament than we had in 1945. When all the results were known, we had a majority of six throughout the whole country and I hope no one will accuse me of immodesty for saying that the 1950 Labour Government was as the direct result of the efforts of the Labour Party and its supporters throughout Wales, because if we had not shown our gains there would have been a majority of two and it is doubtful if we could have formed a Government.

Party Colours

Having unified the Labour Party in Wales, the Executive Committee gave attention to the question of what colours were to be worn by members and supporters during Election Campaigns. I can do no better than quote from a report submitted to and approved by the Annual Meeting in 1951.

> From time to time attempts have been made with a view of securing uniformity concerning Labour Party colours at election times. Efforts have not proved successful for a variety of reasons, but further suggestions have again been received from various quarters asking that another attempt should be made. We therefore communicated with constituency parties to ascertain what colours or sets of colours were being used at election times. The result of our enquiries show that seven sets of colours were used by our Labour Parties in Wales, six of which were also used by other political parties throughout the Principality. We asked our constituency parties if they would be agreeable for the Regional Council Executive Committee to decide on a colour or a combination of colours to cover the Labour Party in Wales. Out of thirty six constituencies thirty one answered in the affirmative, three in the negative and two did not reply. We therefore recommend that your Executive Committee be given power to decide upon a colour or set of colours to be used by the Labour Party throughout Wales.

The Executive Committee therefore decided in favour of a set of colours made up as follows, red, yellow and green, and at that time our action drew public comment, "that the Labour Party in Wales had decided in favour of colours indicating STOP, CAUTION, and GO". I immediately made a public statement accepting the interpretation to our colours. The Labour Party would always be prepared to Stop when necessary and then be cautious, and know when to GO. I went on to explain that the real meaning of the colours we had chosen was red for the blood of the Martyrs, yellow for the Rising Sun of Enlightenment, and green for Liberty.

Prior to the acceptance of this set of colours there was a certain amount of confusion here in Wales and as I travelled from constituency to constituency it was necessary for me to carry several colours in my bag and on arrival at a particular constituency I would see what colour or colours were being worn by our supporters and then take from my bag the appropriate colour. Indeed the colour red was favoured and worn by some of our workers but in at least one constituency the colour red was worn by the Liberals. The acceptance of the set of colours reduced the chance of finding myself wearing the colours worn by an opponent. So it was for more reasons than one a very good thing that agreement had been reached on the colours to be worn by the Labour Party in Wales during Election campaigns.

It was fairly obvious that the Government with a majority of six could not stand the strain for a long period. Therefore, after holding off the opponents for twelve months, the Labour Government decided to call another General Election. It must be admitted that this placed not only a heavy responsibility but also a great burden on the finances of constituency parties.

We in Wales were determined to do all within our power to secure the return of another Labour Government but unfortunately this was not to be and throughout the country we were badly beaten. It was of some consolation to our supporters to know that at the end of the campaign we finished up with two more seats than we had following the 1945 election. We now lost Barry and Conway but gained Angelsey and Merioneth. The voting in Wales was as follows:

Labour	926,127
Conservatives and Supporters	471,269
Liberals	116,821
Welsh Nationalists	10,920
Communists	2,948
Independent	1,643
Total votes cast	1,529,728

In Wales 84.1% of the electors recorded their votes and throughout the whole country 80.5% of the electorate used their votes.

From the above figures it will be noticed that the Labour votes throughout Wales remained loyal but in other parts of Britain many must have been influenced by the tremendous amount of propaganda directed against the Labour Government.

12

The Wales and Monmouthshire Industrial Estates Company
and the Representation of the People Bill 1948

At the 1948 Annual Meeting of the Council of Labour it was reported that very serious consideration was being given to the industrial aspects of Labour Party policy throughout the Principality. There was in existence an Industrial Estates Company which had developed from what had been known as the Treforest Trading Estates Company, which had come into being just prior to the 1939-45 War. In our discussions with the TUC Advisory Committee agreement had been reached on the need to prepare a case for the re-organisation of the Estates Company. We consulted with the Welsh Parliamentary Labour Group who invited us to prepare a memorandum indicating the kind of re-organisation we had in mind. This was carried out and a joint deputation of the Council of Labour and Members of Parliament waited upon the then President of the Board of Trade, Mr Harold Wilson. We were invited to meet him a second time after he, along with others involved, would have time to consider all the points raised by the deputation. In support of our case a full enquiry had been strongly recommended by the Select Committee on Estimates into the managerial structure and results of the Trading Estates Companies concerned with the erection of factories in the Development Areas including Wales. The report of the Select Committee dated 10th May 1947, was quoted by us in support of our case. Serious doubts had been expressed by the Labour Movement particularly in South Wales as to whether the Government was really getting value for the money it was spending. The principle whereby the Estates Company had become the Board of Trade's agent for the erection of factories was part and parcel of the very poor machine handed over from the Churchill Government in 1945. The criticism in the main came from those districts where there were large numbers of unemployed people, including many disabled miners and others. There was great delay in the construction of a number of small factories for the employment of those suffering as a result of silicosis and such delay had been damaging to the reputation of the Labour Government. Part of our case called for a proper balance to be established between the multiple sites for a group of factories with their call for material and services and those single factories which were planned to be near the localities where the unemployed people lived. It was contended that it would be in the interest of the people to pursue a policy of erecting small single factories where needed, instead of concentrating on large sites where a number of factories would be built and thus cause a strain on many of our public services including transport. It did not follow that the policy applied during the war years was applicable now in peace time. Drastic re-organisation was called for because of the method of the over-centralised Trading Estates Company of trying to deal with the whole of Wales from an office in Treforest. It was also felt that some of management had very little experience of industrial organisation and of the requirements of local authorities and it was therefore desirable that new blood should be introduced at an early date into the management of the Estates Company. Our memorandum said:

> An organisation based at Treforest as it is at present cannot deal with the factory requirements for the whole of Wales. There has been a long standing failure of the Treforest Trading Estate to give representation on the Estate Board to workers and persons with progressive views. A better qualified and more active Executive is required for the Welsh Region who can give adequate time to the job. The present Board has no direct contact with the Industrial Movement in Wales and we therefore submit the following recommendations:
>
> 1 That the Board of Trade shall be the responsible Government Department for the entire development of industry in Wales.
> 2 That the President of the Board of Trade shall be the responsible Minister for the appointments to the Board comprising of the Chairman, and twelve other members having interest in Wales. The Minister shall make the appointments on the following basis — three from Industry and Commerce, three from the Trade Unions, one from County Councils, one from Municipal Corporations (County Boroughs) one from the Urban District Councils. There shall also be three Advisory Committees set up, one for East Wales, one for West Wales and one for North Wales and each of these to have a member on the Board.
> 3 That a Consultant from a Government Department shall be available at all times to the Board.
> 4 That the new body shall be known as the Wales and Monmouthshire Trading Estate Development Board.

The Government did not accept the whole of our recommendations but did accept the need for re-organisation of the Trading Estate Company with a broader representation including three members from the trade union movement and members from industry. No member of the Board received any remuneration for his services nor indeed payment for attending meetings of the Board, which were held frequently. In about 1962 the then Tory Government decided it was time for a change and, without giving reasons, appointed almost a completely new Board, with members to be paid for their services. Needless to say, though I had served twelve or fourteen years on the Board, I was not now re-appointed.

I must confess I enjoyed my service as a member of the Board and it is only fair to say that party politics did not enter into our discussions, but we had plenty of fun and leg pulling, for example when the Chairman, who was a prominent member of the Tory Party, chaired our meetings wearing a red tie!

In 1948 the Boundary Commission for Wales published its recommendations for the re-distribution of Parliamentary Seats. The proposed changes were not very great and the main changes were as follows. The University Seat was abolished, as indeed it was in the other parts of Britain. Wales, however, was to continue to have thirty-six Parliamentary Seats, the same number as it had including the one for the University. Flintshire was to have an additional seat and there were changes in Caernarfonshire. The number of seats in that county were to remain the same but the boundaries were adjusted. Up until 1948, there was a seat for the county and also one for the boroughs within the county, the latter the seat that had been held by Lloyd George. The seat for the boroughs was to be abolished and the county was to be divided into two parts with a seat for each. There were also slight changes in the county of Carmarthenshire where a part of the Llanelli constituency was taken away and added on to the seat of Carmarthen. In order to make these recommendations effective a Bill known as the Representation of the People Bill was promoted. This also made residential qualification the only qualification for the Parliamentary franchise. The Bill also specified that there should be published two registers of electors per year. The maximum expenses permitted in support of any candidate at a Parliamentary Election were to be a basic figure of £450 plus 1½d per elector on the register in a county constituency and £450 plus 1d per elector in a borough constituency. The Bill also laid down that County Council Elections should be held in the month of April and all other local government elections, including boroughs, in May. It will, therefore, be noted that 1948 was a particularly busy year when so many changes took place on the political and industrial front as far as Wales was concerned.

13

All Wales Labour Rally

In the little town of Newtown in the County of Montgomeryshire which is mid way between North and South Wales in the heart of the Principality where Robert Owen the great social reformer was born, stands a 1914-18 war time aircraft hangar used as a pavilion for big singing festivals, capable of accommodating 4,000 people. It is an excellent centre for a rally of the Labour Movement in Wales. In 1948, the Montgomeryshire Labour Party decided to organise its own public meeting and a procession through the town to the pavilion. The speaker was Mr. A. V. Alexander, First Lord of the Admiralty in the Labour Government. Unfortunately it was a very wet day and after a short meeting in the local Church graveyard in memory of Robert Owen the procession wended its way through the town and on to the pavilion led by A. V. Alexander, who like many others got soaked to the skin. A. V. was not a young man at that time and much credit is due to him for the way in which he walked at the head of the procession on that particular day. Following the success of the first rally it was decided that the Welsh Regional Council of Labour should take over the job of organising future rallies in Newtown and each was to be run as an 'All Wales Labour Rally.' Much credit was due to the Labour party members in Newtown and District for their services and the success of their efforts. Therefore in 1949, on the first Saturday in July, the first All Wales Labour Rally was held in Newtown. The speaker was Mr Herbert Morrison. Lord President of the Council, who was very popular in Wales because of his understanding of the people and his readiness to help. It was a tremendous rally with 5,000 people endeavouring to get into a pavilion which would really accommodate 4,000. There were hundreds standing and many outside to whom the proceedings were relayed. This kind of rally continued for several years and the speakers included, Mr. C. R. Attlee, the Prime Minister; Mr. Chuter Ede, MP; Mr. Morgan Phillips, Secretary of the Labour Party; Mr. Hugh Gaitskell, MP; Mr. Jim Griffiths, MP, the much loved representative of the people of Wales; and Mr Aneurin Bevan, MP, who was without doubt an outstanding orator and one who loved the enthusiasm of a well attended Labour Party rally. This particular rally was addressed by Aneurin in 1953 during the time of a Tory Government which gave Aneurin an opportunity to attack the Tories who were and have been our main opposition in Wales. Aneurin was on top form and his speech caused so much cheering that it almost raised the roof off the pavilion. At the end of the rally, Aneurin called for "three cheers for an early General Election." He led the cheering by calling out "hip hip hooray." The cheering was something never heard before in the quiet town of Newtown. As we left the platform I said to Aneurin, "And what will happen if we get an early General Election?" He laughed and said, "We will have a damn good hiding, Cliff!" These rallies were great occasions for the Labour Party because supporters travelled from all parts of Wales, some travelling over one hundred miles. At the rally the main speaker would be accompanied by leaders of the Labour Party, the Trade Union Congress and the Co-operative Movement and a visit would be paid to the graveyard where Robert Owen was buried and, there, tribute would be paid to the memory of such a wonderful Socialist. The rally itself would be conducted in real Welsh tradition in the singing of appropriate hymns which would create the right atmosphere for the speakers and then we would always end the rally by the singing of the Welsh National Anthem.

In 1954 the Welsh Regional Council of Labour with the full co-operation of the National Executive Committee of the Labour Party published a Policy Document in readiness for the 1955 General Election. This was a little green pamphlet entitled *Labour's Policy for Wales.* Here I quote a few of its passages on 'Cultural Life within the Principality'. "Labour affirms its determination to do all within its power to assist in the preservation of the Welsh Language and the distinctive culture of Wales. It recalls with pride the positive achievements of the Labour Government of 1945-1951 in this field." It was for instance, the late Ellen Wilkinson who, as Labour's Minister of Education, who set up the Welsh Joint Education Committee which is now so effectively co-ordinating the efforts of Education Authorities within the Principality. Similarly it was her successor in office, the late George Tomlinson, who declared the support of the Labour Party for the movement to set up Welsh Language Schools in many parts of Wales. These are just a few instances of the many actions which Labour took when in power to support the Welsh people in our attempt to safeguard our distinctive heritage. "Labour looks forward to the day when it can in consultation with the elected representatives of Wales take further action to strengthen the cultural life of our small Nation, so renowned for its literary, musical and religious activities. The Labour Party is confident of success if only because of the large number of distinguished Welsh men and women which it includes in its ranks and among its leaders."

Other parts of our 1954 Policy Statement are quoted herewith.

1 Economic Development

The programme for expansion at home for example includes measures to improve the efficiency of the fuel and power industries, including coal, and to provide a balanced industrial structure which will ensure full employment and at the same time reduce our dependence on overseas supplies of food and raw materials. . .

Since the end of the war, more than 100,000 new jobs have been created in Wales as a result of new factory building. This programme will be vigorously pursued. . .

An important contribution will be made through the investment programmes of the nationalised industries. In all, over £100 million will be spent under the National Coal Board's 15 year plan. Large investment projects are also being undertaken by the Gas and Electricity Industries. . .

Labour is pledged to restore the iron and steel industry to public ownership and will pay particular attention to the employment problems arising from the modernisation of the tinplate and steel sheet industry in West Wales. . .

The employment of the disabled presents special problems in Wales. Labour will review the operation of the Grenfell and Remploy schemes and will take

80

steps to see that needs of the disabled are adequately and suitably met. In this connection, account will be taken of the recommendations of the Council for Wales and Monmouthshire and consideration will be given to the possibilities of encouraging the employment of disabled persons by an extended programme of factory building and through the conditional placing of Government orders.

2 Rural Wales

The Reports of the Council for Wales and Monmouthshire have drawn attention to the great need of rural Wales for more housing, water supply, sewerage, better roads and gas and electricity supplies. Labour will examine the Council's recommendations in the light of its own proposals in the policy statement *"Challenge to Britain."*

Labour's policy is also designed to help the farming industry and the rural areas by ensuring that extra fixed capital of all kinds is available for building, drainage and water supply schemes. Further, steps will be taken to see that farmers can obtain easier and cheaper credit facilities for their working capital.

3 Cultural Life

Labour affirms its determination to do all in its power to assist in the preservation of the Welsh language and the distinctive culture of Wales.

It was, for instance, the late Ellen Wilkinson who, as Labour's Minister of Education, set up the Welsh Joint Education Committee which is now so effectively co-ordinating the efforts of the education authorities of the Principality. Similarly it was her successor in office, the late George Tomlinson, who declared the support of the Labour Government for the movement to set up Welsh language schools in many parts of Wales.

These are instances of the many concrete actions which Labour took, when it had the power, to support the Welsh people in their attempts to safeguard their distinctive heritage. Labour looks forward to the day when it can, in consultation with the elected representatives of Wales take further action to strengthen the cultural life of a small nation, so renowned for its literary, musical and religious activities. The Labour Party is confident of success if only because of the large number of distinguished Welsh men and women which it includes in its ranks and indeed among its leaders.

4 Administrative Devolution

Many Government departments have separated their Welsh functions and have established special offices for Wales. These include the Ministries of Health, Education, National Insurance, Agriculture, Housing and Local Government.

Labour will consider the possibility of further measures of administrative devolution and is sympathetic to the proposals of the Council for Wales and Monmouthshire that *(a)* the Welsh activities of the Agricultural Land Service and the National Agricultural Advisory Service should be brought within the administrative responsibility of the Welsh Department of Agriculture; and *(b)* that the headquarters and the office of the Permanent Secretary of the Welsh Department of Education should be in Wales and not in London.

5 Parliamentary Arrangements

The Labour Party proposes that there should be a Minister for Welsh Affairs, with a seat in the Cabinet. The Labour Party will also review the existing arrangements for the examination of Welsh affairs by Welsh Members of Parliament, with a view to providing the maximum opportunity for the detailed and effective scrutiny of all legislation and administration affecting Wales.

Labour will seek to allocate more Parliamentary time for the discussion of Welsh affairs. In addition to the Welsh day voted to the White Paper on Government action in Wales and Monmouthshire, a day might be set aside to the discussion of the report of the Council for Wales and Monmouthshire, or for any subjects which the Welsh members desire to raise.

Finally, Labour will revise the constitution of the Council for Wales and Monmouthshire with the purpose of making it a more representative and more effective organ of Welsh opinion.

14

The General Election of 1955 and
Labour Representation

In Great Britain and Northern Ireland 76.8% of the total electorate voted, but in Wales the percentage of electors who voted was higher. The necessary information which is very revealing is as follows:

Welsh Boroughs	Total Electorate	536,755
	Votes Recorded	411,401
	Percentage Polled	79.9
Welsh Counties	Total Electorate	1,264,462
	Votes Recorded	1,015,318
	Percentage Polled	80.3
Whole of Wales	Total Electorate	1,811,217
	Total who voted	1,433,719
	Percentage	79.1

Not only does Wales poll a higher percentage than the remainder of Great Britain and Northern Ireland but it is significant, and should be noted, that in Wales the county constituencies, some of them covering vast rural areas, poll a higher percentage than the compact borough constituencies. In this particular General Election the Labour Party did not gain or lose any seats in Wales but held on to its 27 seats and our opponents held 9 seats.

In this period the Welsh Council of Labour had to defend its position on several occasions and I mention a couple of examples as recorded in our Annual Reports.

British Broadcasting Corporation (Wales) and the Labour Party

The Welsh Council of Labour had over a period contended that the BBC in Wales was biased and showed favour to the Welsh Nationalist Party. The Convention which was held in Llandrindod Wells, mentioned on an earlier page, brought matters into the open. I quote from the Annual Report on the Welsh Council of Labour dated the 14th April 1950:

> We made representations to the BBC Wales complaining that the BBC Welsh News Bulletin had shown anti-Labour and pro-Welsh Nationalist political bias. A deputation from your Executive Committee met Mr A. Oldfield-Davies, Regional Controller of the BBC on two separate occasions and during the discussions evidence was produced by the deputation relative to our complaints but our Regional Controller was not prepared to admit political bias. We therefore communicated with Sir William Haley Director General of the BBC London, inviting him to institute an Official Enquiry at which the Council of

Labour would be prepared to give evidence to substantiate its complaints. Sir William informed us that the Governors of the BBC had come to the conclusion that there was no evidence of bias on the part of the BBC in Wales against the Labour Party and in favour of the Welsh Nationalists, and therefore could not grant our request for an enquiry. We were therefore not given an opportunity to submit evidence to substantiate our complaints. Sir William Haley, however did admit to errors made by the BBC (A) employment as a local correspondent of a full time official of the Welsh Nationalist Party, (B) The employment of the General Secretary of the Welsh Nationalist Party to give the report of the Llandrindod Convention.

The two officers referred to are not journalists. Even though we were not granted an enquiry we are convinced that the kind of errors admitted by the BBC will not be repeated. The Welsh Parliamentary Labour Group was kept informed of our negotiations with the BBC and subsequent results.

Hospital Management Committees

During November 1955, it came to the notice of the Executive Committee that the Welsh Regional Hospital Board had decided to invite the Conservative Party in Wales to nominate for seats on Hospital Management Committees throughout the Principality. This matter was immediately taken up by officers of the Regional Council of Labour and they had discussion with officers of the Regional Hospital Board, following which a letter was received from the Hospital Board inviting the Labour Party in Wales to nominate for seats on all Hospital Management Committees. The Regional Council of Labour thought it was completely wrong for Political Parties to nominate for such seats and passed the following resolution which was sent on to the Regional Hospital Board:

a   That we consider it undesirable for Political Parties as such to be represented on Hospital Management Committees, and therefore we do not wish to submit nominations.

b   This is an entirely new procedure, as far as we know, for any Political Party to be invited to nominate.

c   We ask the General Purposes Committee of the Regional Hospital Board to receive a deputation from the Regional Council of Labour so that we might state our case for our non-acceptance of the invitation to nominate.

d   The matter to be reported to the TUC and the Welsh Parliamentary Labour Group.

e   The deputation to wait upon the General Purposes Committee of the Regional Hospital Board shall be the Officers of the Regional Council of Labour together with Dr K. G. Pendse.

In December 1955, we received a letter from the Regional Hospital Board intimating that they did not wish our deputation to attend, and that they had now decided to withdraw the invitation which had been sent to the Conservative Party seeking nominations for seats on Hospital Management Committees. These notes are taken from the Annual Report of the Executive Committee of the Regional Council of Labour May 26th 1956.

Anti-Apartheid Protests

The Regional Council of Labour, in co-operation with the South Wales Area of the National Union of Mineworkers, conducted an Anti-Apartheid Campaign throughout South Wales during the whole of 1957. Platforms at all our meetings were used to expose the policy of the South African Government who were conducting a policy of apartheid in the selection of players to represent South Africa in all forms of sport. We were aware that a South African Cricket team would be playing against Glamorgan during the August Bank Holiday at Cardiff Arms Park. We, therefore, appealed for our members and supporters to boycott this match in protest over the policy of the South African Government. During the match itself a number of us demonstrated by walking up and down Westgate Street Cardiff, carrying banners displaying slogans such as "They're All White Jack," "Apartheid isn't Cricket", "There is only one Race - the Human Race". We also distributed leaflets explaining the reasons for our protest and appealing for people not to enter the playing field. Our demonstration was quite peaceful and we found a great deal of sympathy and support from a large number of people. There was a radio commentary on the match by Mr Peter West and you can imagine our delight when late in the afternoon we heard coming over the radio the comment that the crowd at the match was disappointing because a much bigger crowd was expected. Those of us who had carried banners throughout the day went home well pleased with our efforts. We had just one regret inasmuch as our efforts must have meant a loss of gate money to Glamorgan Cricket Club.

Training Sessions

It was my custom to run week-end schools for election workers throughout the Principality in between elections and in fact as soon as one General Election was over, preparations would be made in order to organise in readiness for any eventuality. During 1957 one of these schools was held in Coleg Harlech, this being a favourite of ours over several years. During Saturday afternoon it was our practice to have a free period with no lectures until after the evening meal. On this particular occasion, arrangements were made to provide transport so that all attending the school could be taken to a special place of interest. So off we went in a number of motor cars down along the coast road. On reaching Llanbedr we turned left along a road taking us to Cwm-Nant-Col, which nestled high up between some hills. I had been to this place on a number of occasions so it was not unknown to me. I, therefore, thought it would be of special interest to those attending our school. We parked our cars and approached a small chapel which is known as 'Salem': a picture of it is displayed in many homes throughout Wales. The chapel and the caretaker's house are both under the one roof. I knew the procedure was to call at the caretaker's house to ask for the key to enter the little chapel. I received the key and the caretaker informed me that she was going out shopping and asked if I would slip the key in through her letter box when we would be leaving the little chapel. As we entered 'Salem', we looked around and then got together in the pews near a little organ. We soon found some hymn books and spent some little time singing hymns and having a wonderful time. We took a collection and left it on a plate on a small table as our small contribution. However as we sang hymns I quite unintentionally rested my arm on the frail music rest on the organ and the weight of my arm broke it. This

85

caused me much embarrassment, so on returning the key I placed through the letter box a note offering my apology, giving my name and address asking that a new music rest should be purchased and the account for same to be sent to me. In about a week's time I received a lovely letter from the caretaker asking me not to worry about what had happened. She said that in any case there was no need to purchase a new music rest because her husband had repaired the one which had been damaged and it was now as good as new. There would be no account for me to pay but she added a note saying how grateful they of the church were for what we had left on the collection plate.

As I stated earlier, I had been to 'Salem' on a number of occasions but this is the visit I remember most, perhaps because of my little mishap and the wonderful way in which it ended. As I look upon the picture of 'Salem' which is in my home, I am reminded of the many men and women who worshipped there and who by their example helped to hand down to us the heritage which is ours today. Our visit to 'Salem' enhanced our weekend School and I am sure that those who were with me at that time will now look back with a certain amount of pleasure.

It should be noted that the Wales Tourist Board is now particularly interested in 'Salem' which became famous when painted by S. Cernew Vosper who used the little chapel and its congregation as models. This made 'Salem' a national treasure, visited by so many tourists from all parts of the world. The original painting hangs in the Lever Collection in Liverpool and copies can be seen in homes not only in Wales but in many parts of the world.

15

The Carmarthen By-Election

Late in 1956 news came of the death of Sir Rhys Hopkin Morris, the much respected and very capable Liberal Member of Parliament for the Carmarthen Constituency. During the 1955 General Election, in a three cornered fight — Liberal, Labour and Welsh Nationalist — the Liberals held the seat with a majority of 3,333 over Labour.

This vacancy presented us with a very interesting situation because it was held by the Liberals with the support of the Tory Party and if a Tory candidate would be nominated the seat could be won by Labour. However, we had no candidate selected and the Liberals played right into our court by delaying the by-election. Inasmuch as it was a Liberal seat, it was left to the Liberal Whip in the House of Commons to decide when to move the Writ for the calling of the by-election. If the Liberals had decided on an early election, they might have caught us unprepared, because we would have to hurry the selection of a candidate which would not be in our interest. It was rumoured that the Tories were going to put forward a candidate so the Liberals had to be very careful in whatever action they cared to take and in all probability the discussions between the Liberals and the Tories were responsible for the delay. However, both these Parties appeared to have come to an agreement that the Liberals would select a candidate who would satisfy the Tories and one whom they could support though he would carry the Liberal flag. In the meantime we set about selecting a candidate and this caused very keen competition with the final choice between Lady Megan Lloyd George (who had come over to the Labour Party from the Liberals following the previous General Election) and Mr John Morris a young man who lived in the adjoining constituency of Cardiganshire.

I shall never forget the selection conference held in Church House, Carmarthen, which was full to capacity with delegates from trade unions, and Labour Party organisations. The conference was tense as delegates sat and listened to the addresses from the nominees each one claiming to be able to represent the Labour Party in this particular constituency. When the final ballot vote was taken it was revealed that Lady Megan had won the candidature and the support of the majority of delegates. The delegates then on a show of hands gave an unanimous vote in favour of Lady Megan and promised to work for her during the election. The nominees were then invited to the platform and it was announced by the chairman that Lady Megan had been selected to fight the by-election on behalf of the Labour Party subject to confirmation by the National Executive Committee of the Labour Party. It was not our custom to announce the final figures when selecting a candidate though they were of course known to the delegates when the result was declared.

On the following morning I met Lady Megan along with Mr Desmond Donnelly on the Railway Station, Carmarthen, on her way to London.

She looked at me with a twinkle in her eye and said, "That was a very near thing at the conference yesterday, Cliff." Someone had given her the figures showing she had won the candidature by a single vote over Mr John Morris. I asked her to forget about the single vote and reminded her that on a show of hands the conference gave to her a unanimous vote. However, I was convinced and am still convinced that Lady Megan was the most suitable person to fight this particular seat and I could not think of anyone else who would give us hope of victory.

The constituency party invited me to act as Election Agent and Lady Megan expressed her pleasure and satisfaction. I immediately arranged to meet the constituency party and formed a campaign committee to organise our support throughout the constituency. The very first thing I had to do was to convince our own members that with their help this pending by-election could be won for Labour. Carmarthen is a huge parliamentary constituency and much of it is rural, though in the south east of the county there is an industrial belt. This constituency was also known for its high poll in all elections and in the 1955 General Election it recorded a poll of 85.1%. That figure would take some beating but I advised the campaign committee that I wanted to obtain a still higher percentage poll in order to achieve victory. I explained the kind of campaign to be conducted and was in a favourable position to be able to allocate certain people to be responsible for particular districts. I was assisted by Miss Megan Roach and Mr Hubert Morgan, Assistant Organisers, who with others made a very valuable contribution during the whole of the campaign.

Much of our activities were strange to local Labour Party members who had not experienced this kind of campaign. They had succeeded in obtaining an 85.1% poll without any special kind of organisation on their part. Though I was introducing new methods I had to make sure to carry the local supporters with me and it was, therefore, necessary to keep them advised of my actions and the reasons. I secured campaign committee rooms in the centre of Carmarthen and also committee rooms with telephones in various parts of the Constituency. The support coming forward was wonderful and this inspired confidence when members of the Labour Party and Trade Unions volunteered their services and confessed that they had not been active during previous elections. I took advantage of the fact that the Liberals had selected a candidate who was acceptable to the Tories. I contended that he could not be a real Liberal and we should endeavour to win over the radicals who had in the past voted Liberal. This suggestion shocked some of our supporters until it was explained very fully to them that quite a number of people who support us at every election were radicals and our task is to win support for our cause. Arrangements were made for Lady Megan to come into the county and meet the election workers. She would also visit parts of the constituency for the purpose of meeting groups of influential members of the public, including the road man in the rural part of the county because he was an important person in our campaign; he would during his working days meet a large number of people and a word from him would be helpful. Lady Megan was not to commence her public campaign for the time being because we knew from past experience that a long campaign can, on the final days, lose its impact and we had to avoid this happening. Our organisation was quiet but busy, arranging meeting places, securing promises from speakers and collecting cash in order to pay our way. I was then unfortunate to be laid aside with a slipped disc and in much pain but from my home in Penarth, with a telephone near at hand, I was able to give directions in preparation for our public campaign. Miss Sarah Barker, who was our National Agent, arrived in Carmarthen to offer advice and guidance which meant her keeping in touch with me over the telephone. I was forbidden by my doctor to leave my bed and he called in a consultant who in turn confirmed what I had been told by my local doctor. I was measured for a belt to wear and was told that it would take some time before it would be available for me. After a few days I was able to get out of bed and sit near to the telephone and, though confined to my home, my heart was in Carmarthen where there was so much interesting work to be carried out. I received a telephone call from Miss Barker asking me if I could get down to Carmarthen, where I could spend the whole of my time sitting in an armchair in the Central Committee Room, which would give her and the local workers much satisfaction. I therefore persuaded my local doctor to allow me to go, after he made it clear that I had to strap myself with some kind of belt or corset. I got in touch with some of my friends in industry who arranged for some very large dunlop cushions to be sent to our committee rooms in Carmarthen for my use in a big armchair. I obtained from a neighbour the loan of a maternity corset which I fastened tightly around my body and off I went to Carmarthen by train, to conduct the campaign which I had planned, and I returned to Cardiff weekly for special treatment. Lady Megan had by now arrived in the constituency and had taken up accommodation in the Royal Ivy Bush Hotel. I stayed in a small guest house and so did Miss Roach and Miss Barker when she was visiting us, but for obvious reasons she could not spend much time with us.

The Liberals in the House of Commons had moved the Writ and it had been arranged that the election would take place on the 28th February. I should mention here that a new register of electors would be published on the 16th February but we succeeded in persuading the Returning Officer to have the register published a few days earlier in order to give both sides an opportunity to go through it. This meant we were going to fight this election with an up-to-date register and the maximum number of electors being available to record their votes.

The time for nomination of candidates was approaching and agents were securing signatures in support of the nominees. All this was well in hand as far as we were concerned and I paid one of my weekly visits to Cardiff for treatment and was to spend the night at home in Penarth which is about four miles from Cardiff. I received a telephone call asking me to return that very night because a serious difficulty had arisen which required my attention without delay.

I reached Carmarthen very late in the night and was told that Lady Megan was not prepared to include her full christian names on the nomination paper. It had come to the notice of our workers in the Central Committee Rooms that the Liberals were seeking legal advice with a view of trying to get Lady Megan's nomination forms declared void if it did not contain her full christian names. The following morning, accompanied by Mr Hubert Morgan, I met Lady Megan in her hotel and explained to her that the nomination form asked for all christian names as well as the surname of the person nominated. I had not known until that morning that one of her christian names was Arfon but apparently it was seldom used and Lady Megan did not wish to use it. She explained that she would have a word with the Returning Officer and tell him that she had never used the name Arfon when contesting previous elections. I pointed out to her that no one in Angelsey where she had been a Member of Parliament had lodged a complaint, but if the Liberals now complained the Returning Officer would be placed in a very difficult position. If he declared her nomination form to be void, it would be too late for us to do anything about it. That was a risk we ought not to take and I would not wish to appeal to any court on such an issue. Lady Megan then said, "I will do whatever you wish, Cliff", so the name Arfon was included much to the annoyance of the Liberals. On leaving the hotel Mr Hubert Morgan expressed great surprise that I was able to get Lady Megan to agree to my suggestion, I replied saying, "I was not very surprised because I had always found her to be helpful and ready to be advised by me as her Election Agent." This was a tremendously exciting and invigorating election campaign and though in much pain I enjoyed every minute of it. I said earlier on that I stayed in a small guest house, but what I did not say was that Miss Megan Roach came to my room every morning and fastened my electric razor to an electric light bulb socket which was too high for me to reach, especially as I could not risk standing on a chair. Megan would also tie my shoe laces because I could not bend. This procedure continued throughout the campaign and Megan, bless her, did it without complaint. Just before the end of the special activities in the Carmarthen constituency, my belt arrived and I was able to feel a little more comfortable.

This by-election was fought very fiercely with three candidates in the field representing the Liberals, the Welsh Nationalists and the Labour Party. The Tory Government had blundered very badly over the Suez Canal and we were determined to attack the Tory record and make it as embarrassing as possible for the Liberal candidate who had Tory support. He surely could not condone what had happened and yet if he criticised the Tory Government he would lose the support of the local Tory Party so he was in a very invidious position.

We made the most of the situation but there came a time about two thirds of the way through the campaign when it became necessary to advise all our speakers including our candidate to give up talking about Suez and deal with matters directly affecting the people in the constituency. Carmarthen is a great milk producing area so milk was now to be the subject for discussion on every platform. I have found in my experience that, though Foreign Affairs are important, the electors are more concerned with what is happening on the home front. Our campaign was going well and according to plan while our workers continued to have plenty of fun.

One of the highlights was a public meeting in the Market Hall in the town of Carmarthen. It had never been known before for a meeting to be arranged in such a place as the Market Hall because it was such a vast building and our opponents were amazed at what they considered to be our audacity in organising a meeting with accommodation for 3,000 people. We were fortunate in having as our guest speaker the Rt Hon Aneurin Bevan and felt confident that he would draw the supporters — and many of the opponents — because he was such an attractive speaker. We sold tickets at one shilling each and filled the Market Hall' to capacity but the Liberals throughout the campaign threatened us with legal action on the very least pretence and we were advised that they were seeking legal advice on their complaint that we were expecting the electors to pay one shilling for a ticket so that they could gain admission to what was called a public meeting. In order to avoid any trouble and to satisfy the authorities that we were not wishing to prevent any elector from attending I advised all our stewards not to refuse entry to any person who came to one of the doors of the hall even though the said person had no ticket.

It was our custom to arrange for hymn singing at our election meetings, and particularly in places like Carmarthen, so you can just imagine what it was like to have 3,000 people singing their favourite Welsh hymns. I have known nothing to compare with this in any other place outside Wales. The singing creates the necessary atmosphere for the speakers and it also gives a feeling of fellowship to those taking part and after all our Party claims to be one of fellowship. We closed the meeting with the singing of the Welsh National Anthem (Mae Hen Wlad Fy Nhadau).

The meeting was a huge success and gave confidence to our supporters and at the same time caused tension in the ranks of our opponents. The Liberals were continually pressurised by the Tories and on one occasion they were heard quarrelling openly in the market in the presence of farmers and cattle dealers: this was all good for us.

The Labour Candidate's Central Committee Room was a beehive of activity and many callers came along wanting to know how the campaign was going and enquired from us our forecast of the result. We had quite a lot of valuable information brought to our Central Committee Room from the Liberal-Tory camp which helped us in our approach to many local questions.

I must say that throughout the whole of the campaign I found the Liberal candidate to be courteous and polite but I came to the conclusion that he did not have his heart in the fight: he did not like the pressure put upon him by the local Tories.

91

The Welsh Nationalist candidate was very able, charming, courteous, polite, and a very good speaker, but appeared to be pushed too hard by the leaders of her Party. Her qualities led to much speculation concerning the possible result of the poll. Several Members of the Labour Party, including some Members of Parliament, came to me and declared that this particular Welsh Nationalist Candidate would take a lot of votes away from the Labour Candidate and allow the Liberal to win the election. It was, of course, known that in previous by-elections the Welsh Nationalist candidate would take votes from us particularly in a safe Labour constituency. This, however, was not a Labour Seat and there was being conducted a real political battle and we continually made it clear that the real fight was between Labour and Tory under the name Liberal. I remember one of our national leaders telling me that the Welsh Nationalist candidate would poll more than 10,000 votes and that would mean that we could not win the election. I readily acknowledged the ability, charm and personality of the Welsh Nationalist candidate but I could not bring myself to believe that she could possibly poll more than 10,000 votes and I made it clear to our workers in the Central Committee Room that she would lose her deposit. The way our campaign was being conducted and the information of our progress reaching us from all parts of the constituency convinced me the people of Carmarthen were not going to throw away their votes when there was so much at stake. Our workers had been so wonderful and the kind of campaign conducted gave much confidence to those taking part. However, as we reached the last week of the campaign, so many of our workers having heard how well the Welsh Nationalist candidate was doing and the Liberal gaining support, caused doubt to enter the minds of some of our most faithful workers. A whispering campaign, probably started by one of the Welsh Nationalists, was gaining ground and having its effect on our workers. People called at my Central Committee Room and others telephoned me expressing their doubt in our ability to win this all important seat for the Labour Party.

In fact, during the last couple of days prior to polling day it had got so bad that Miss Barker our National Agent, who again had come down from London, was perturbed because of what she had heard. She asked to see me alone in the committee room. She turned the key in the door and said to me, "I want to know from you not what you hope but what you really believe is going to happen on polling day." Miss Barker continued, "I have met a number of workers, including some of our full-time officers of the Labour Party, who have been frightened by what was happening in our opponents' camp." I replied saying, "I was well aware that many of our own workers had lost faith in themselves and therefore in their ability to win, but believe me we are going to win." Miss Barker then said, "Well you are on your own, Cliff, but, knowing you, I accept your assessment;" The key of the door was again turned and in walked one of our very active workers in the person of Elwyn John, who was a trade union branch official and was engaged in a workshop alongside the river Towy, which flowed peacefully through the constituency and passed quite near the Shire Hall and also the County Hall. Elwyn was very depressed and said to me in the presence of Miss Barker. "Look here, Cliff, we have been led to believe that we were going to win but now I see nothing but defeat for us." Then he came nearer to me and said, "If we lose, I will throw you into the Towy." I remember the late Lord Shepherd, when he was National Agent, telling me, "After every by-election, the National Executive Committee would conduct an inquest and the result was always the same; if we won it was because we had a good candidate but if we lost it was because we had a poor agent." I had conducted many by-elections and was always concerned with running an effective campaign with my eye on polling day. I must say a word about our candidate Lady Megan, she was attractive, charming, very capable, a great political fighter. She had learned so many things from her illustrious father and was in complete control of any platform. I could not wish to have had a better candidate and can say with confidence that I know of no other candidate better able to win Carmarthen for us at that time. I was responsible for planning her work, including her appointments, her visits to see certain people, her public meetings, and so on, and she carried the functions out in great style. She was as we say in Welsh a 'Cariad'. There does not appear to be a word in the English language to convey the same meaning. It was an experience and a great pleasure to act as her Election Agent.

The Counting of the Votes

Polling day was over without any difficulty and we now assembled at the Shire Hall, Carmarthen, at about 9.30 a.m. on the 1st of March, St. David's Day, to witness the counting of the votes. I had arranged that there was no need for Lady Megan to be in attendance until about 11.00 a.m. when she arrived bringing with her coffee and sandwiches. The way the count was conducted was not what I had been accustomed to, but it was very efficient and carried out without any fuss. The ballot papers were counted for each candidate and sorted out into bundles of one thousand and passed up to the Returning Officer who was seated on a platform along with one or two members of his staff. He would record the number of votes for each candidate on a sheet of paper and then place the bundle of ballot papers into an empty ballot box. He would at intervals call the election agents to the platform so that we could see the votes recorded for each candidate. The system I had been accustomed to was that the voting papers for each candidate would be collected into a bundle of fifty, then one hundred, then one thousand. The bundles would then be placed on a large table opposite the name of each candidate. We, the election agents, could then see at a glance how each candidate was standing in relation to the poll. However, as I stated, Carmarthen had its own way and I was quite happy with the arrangements. Lady Megan was sitting on her own in a room quite near to the room where the votes were counted, so at about 11.30 a.m., I went to see her and said quite casually, "I think you are winning." She looked at me and said, "You think, Cliff?" I knew what she meant and gave her a few words of comfort before going back to the count.

The counting of the ballot papers and the recording of the votes for each candidate was rapidly drawing to its close and I, along with the other agents, was invited to the platform to see the exact number of votes recorded for each candidate. As I left the platform the last of the ballot boxes were emptied on to the tables to be checked and counted by the counters. I had arranged with our tellers to have a quick check on the tables because I knew from the records that we wanted about half of the votes from the last boxes to be safe. I went around half of the tables myself and asked my wife to visit the other half and give me a quick estimate. The reports were received and what I had seen gave me complete satisfaction. I went over to Lady Megan, who was in the room now where the votes were counted. I squeezed her hand and said, "You are in, so get ready with your correct speech in readiness for when the count is declared." Lady Megan had told me prior to polling day that she always prepared two short speeches for the day of the counting of the votes, one for if she lost and the other for if she had won.

The Returning Officer in due course declared the result of the Election which was as follows:

Lady Megan Arfon Lloyd George	(Lab)	23,679
John Morgan Davies	(Lib)	20,610
Mrs. J. E. Davies	(Welsh Nat)	5,741
	Lab Majority	3,069

There had been a record poll of 87.5% of the electorate taking part in the poll and this was and still is an all time record for any by-election. The Welsh Nationalist candidate lost her deposit because she did not poll one eighth of the votes recorded. It will also be noted that Lady Megan converted a Liberal majority, in the 1955 General Election, of 3,333 into a Labour majority of 3,069. At the end of the counting of the votes the atmosphere in the room became very tense and on hearing the result it became electrified and outside the Shire Hall were thousands of people waiting in great expectation. The result was declared in the midst of tremendous excitement. Needless to say I was very happy and felt rewarded for keeping my faith in the electors of this constituency. As we were about to leave the Shire Hall, Elwyn John came rushing up the stairway and suddenly caught around me and said, "You have saved the Towy, Cliff"; he remembered what he had told me just before polling day.

Following the declaration of the poll, the candidate, accompanied by a number of supporters in twelve motor cars, made off amid the cheering crowd for a tour of the constituency. This was in every sense a real 'Victory Tour' and I well remember the enthusiastic welcome given to Lady Megan as we travelled along through towns and villages. After travelling for a few hours we arrived in the early evening in a coal mining village of Brynamman all feeling tired and hungry because we had not had any lunch because of all the excitement in the Shire Hall. Anyhow the cars stopped in a street of terraced houses and I got out of the car and spoke to one of the many local residents who came out of their houses to

94

greet us. I asked if there was a cafe in Brynamman where we could have a cup of tea. All members of our party were immediately taken into the homes of these wonderfully hospitable people and provided with refreshments. Lady Megan and I were in the home of a coal miner who was suffering from silicosis, that chronic lung disease caused by inhaling coal dust. His wife had been baking cake which had not long come out of the oven and it smelt beautiful and tasted delicious. We were offered a loaf to take away but obviously the offer could not be accepted but my wife, in declining, asked if she could have the recipe. This was supplied and has been used frequently in our home over the years and the recipe has travelled far and wide and has been used by many of our friends for what we name 'Brynamman Cake.' What we experienced in Brynamman is typical of the hospitality given freely throughout the Principality. This was a wonderful conclusion to a by-election which had been strenuously fought but had brought out many good qualities from our supporters. It is also true to say that in addition to the very hard work there had been much enjoyment with a great deal of laughter. The result was not really achieved by the candidate though she played her part, nor the election agent though he had played his part, the credit for the victory must go to the many active voluntary workers throughout the whole constituency.

There was a sequel to the time I spent in Carmarthen constituency, because when I retired in 1965 I was presented with a suitably inscribed miniature coracle to remind me of the fellowship and comradeship enjoyed during that famous by-election. That was not all. On the Saturday prior to Easter, which was a short time following the by-election, I received a small parcel through the post and on opening it there was a set of gold links with the initials of Lady Megan and my own and the date of the by-election. I was very surprised and very thrilled with this very wonderful present which will remain for all time my very precious possession.

95

16

The Wrexham By-Election, the 1959 General Election and the Festival of Labour

The General Election of 1959

At this General Election the Labour Party in Wales defended twenty seven seats and attacked nine. At the very outset it had to be appreciated that more than 78 per cent of the electorate in Wales voted in the 1955 General Election against the figure of just over 76 per cent for the whole of Britain. Our aim therefore was to encourage our maximum support to come out and poll. This is just what we did and 82.5% of the electorate in Wales voted whereas for the whole of Britain 78.7% of the electorate voted. It was an achievement for us to obtain such a heavy poll from a register of electors which was almost twelve months old. The Labour vote was increased in twenty three of the thirty six constituencies in the Principality, though it must be pointed out that in the main our increases were recorded in the constituencies known as 'safe Labour seats.' In 1955 Labour polled 825,690 votes and in 1959 the Labour vote was increased to 841,447, or an increase of 16,000. The result of the election was that Labour held on to its twenty seven seats. Tory candidates forfeited their deposits in Rhondda East and Rhondda West. The Welsh Nationalist had twenty candidates and forfeited fourteen deposits. The Communist Party had two candidates and forfeited one deposit. There was also an Independent candidate and he lost his deposit.

Secretary of State for Wales

It is only right and proper for me to record how it came about for us to press for the appointment of a Secretary of State for Wales. The Labour Party in the Principality had not been in favour of such an appointment since 1948 when the Council for Wales had been set up and given special responsibility. There had of course been those Members of Parliament, though small in number, who never gave up advocating such an appointment and there were amongst their number a couple who went much farther and openly campaigned in favour of a Parliament for Wales, even though such proposals had been overwhelmingly defeated on a democratic vote at our Annual Conferences. However, the Labour Party made it known that there was no objection to this very small minority expressing their views as long as they made it clear they were speaking for themselves and not for the Labour Party. During 1959 a special committee was appointed to examine the advantages if any in the proposal for the appointment of a Secretary of State for Wales. This committee was representative of the National Executive Committee of the Labour Party, the Parliamentary Labour Party, the Welsh Parliamentary Labour Group and the Welsh Council of Labour under the chairmanship of the Rt Hon Hugh Gaitskell, Leader of the Labour Party. The Committee met several times in a room in the House of Commons and from the very first meeting this subject for discussion was known to be a very emotive one. The Rt Hon Aneurin Bevan, then Deputy Leader of the Labour Party, had never been in favour of the appointment of a Secretary of State for Wales and argued that such appointment could not work because there would be conflict between whoever was appointed and other departmental Ministers of the Crown. This was not his only reason and he therefore argued against such an appointment and at times became very emotional. The Rt Hon Ness Edwards was very much opposed to the appointment of a Secretary of State for Wales and in his argument he underlined many of the things said by Aneurin Bevan.

One of those very much in favour of an appointment was the Rt Hon James Griffiths, who had for many years presented his reasons. He had a personal conviction that it would be in the interest of the people of Wales. He could never understand why Scotland had a Secretary of State but Wales had been denied the right to have one. Here then were great stalwarts in our movement taking different sides on this issue, with other representatives joining in the discussion, but all being kept in order by Hugh Gaitskell. James Griffiths used all his power as a negotiator in an attempt to persuade other members of this committee of the justice of his case. No one could for one moment doubt the sincerity of James Griffiths and yet, on the other hand, there was the powerful case put forward in opposition by Aneurin Bevan who was equally convinced that such an appointment was not necessary.

It was obvious that Mr Hugh Gaitskell was in favour of an appointment and we were now in a situation where different views were expressed by the Leader and Deputy Leader just prior to a General Election. After several meetings of protracted and heated discussion, and at what now turned out to be the final meeting, and right in the middle of a very heated debate, to everyone's surprise, Mr Aneurin Bevan proposed, "That we include in our policy statement, that a Secretary of State for Wales will be appointed."

Without any further discussion the meeting was immediately brought to a close. On leaving the room I turned to Ness Edwards and said, "I cannot understand the complete change of attitude by Aneurin." Ness replied, "If you were a member of this House, Cliff, you would not be surprised at what has taken place this afternoon." I think it fair to say that though James Griffiths had been consistent in his pleadings for the appointment of a Secretary of State for Wales, it was, however, the changed attitude of Aneurin Bevan that caused the Labour Party to agree to such an appointment.

It must be noted that the Labour Party in Wales was not interested in having a Secretary of State for Wales and the last decision on this subject had been taken in 1948 when it was decided by Annual Conference of the Regional Council of the Labour Party that the appointment of a Secretary of State for Wales was not necessary. This point was made known during discussions at this Special Committee and it is unfortunate that some people claim that the decision taken by the Committee was in keeping with the wishes of the Labour Party in Wales. This was not so.

The date of the General Election was known and it was in the interest of the Labour Party that there should be complete agreement between the Leader and the Deputy Leader of our Party, this might have been a reason for Aneurin Bevan's change of attitude.

There was no time to lose so a Conference was convened in Cory Hall Cardiff on Saturday, September 12th, to prepare for the General Election which would be held on Thursday, October 8th, and to receive a report of action taken by the Special Committee in London which meant that a Labour Government would appoint a Secretary of State for Wales. There was no one in our Movement going to rock the boat by contesting what happened in London but this particular kind of conference was not in a position to agree or disagree and were not asked to do so. The decision arrived at by the Special Committee was taken too late to have been included in our Manifesto, which had already been printed. The General Election took place and it was won by the Conservatives which meant that we had failed to win power since 1951. We did not lose any seats in Wales but there were those who thought that by agreeing to the appointment of a Secretary of State for Wales we would win additional seats. So the 1959 General Election resulted in a set back for the Labour Party but the fight between Conservatives and Socialists would continue and we settled down making preparations for the next General Election.

The Wrexham By-Election

In writing about by-elections I decided to commence with Carmarthen because of its vital importance and the special kind of campaign conducted in this particular part of Wales. However, I now move to Wrexham where there was a by-election in 1955, caused through the death of Mr Robert Richards, the much talented and highly respected Labour Member of Parliament. He had been Under-Secretary for India in the Labour Government 1922-24, and again became Member of Parliament for the Wrexham Constituency 1929-31 and then from 1935 to 1955. It was not easy to find a suitable candidate to follow Robert Richards but Mr James Idwal Jones was selected and proved himself to be a very good candidate. He realised that if elected he would be in a rather unique situation because his brother T. W. Jones was the Member of Parliament for Merioneth. Anyhow this was quite a happy by-election apart from the controversy in the Labour Party nationally over the threatened withdrawal of the Whip in the House of Commons from the Rt Hon Aneurin Bevan. This, as was expected, had repercussions in our election campaign organisation. My chief concern at that time was to have a good campaign, which would assure a favourable result and it was therefore important to keep harmony and unity in our ranks, and that these things were in a large measure accomplished. Wrexham was an important constituency with a mixed electorate, with its main town a centre of commerce and business, and the surrounding villages were to some extent industrialised and others were very rural in character. Rightly or wrongly I have always taken the view that election strategy meant dealing with each area

99

or town, or indeed village, as separately in a way which would give the desired result. This meant that speakers had to be selected upon their suitability for town or village and the subject which they were going to place before the electors. For example a speaker who could make out a good case in a coal mining district was not of necessity the automatic choice of person to send into an agricultural village. We took all this into consideration when making an allocation of speakers for various parts of the constituency. I would like to mention one particular village in this constituency. It is Rhosllannerchrugog, rich in Welsh culture, a coal mining village with a socialist background. We could in fact send to this village a speaker who was an academic as long as he knew Socialism and could speak in the language of the villagers who were also steeped in religion. This village was also the rallying point for the whole constituency not for elections only but whenever any campaign was conducted on behalf of the Labour Party. It is worth mentioning that at parliamentary elections there would be an eve of the poll meeting held in this place and always to commence at 8.00 p.m. This by-election was not to be treated differently, so all speakers who were addressing meetings on behalf of the Labour candidate in any part of the constituency, on the eve of the poll, were advised to assemble at the Welfare Hall, Rhosllannerchrugog, after the conclusion of the meetings they were addressing I must confess I was a little nervous thinking that perhaps speakers would arrive at the selected point after the meeting was over. I was assured that there was no need for me to have any fears because the meeting would not finish before midnight. I arrived at the meeting at about 10.00 p.m. and found the hall quite full with many of the women folk carrying flasks of coffee or tea prepared for a long meeting. True to form, the meeting went on until after midnight and in the first hour of the morning the meeting was concluded by the singing of a well known hymn in Welsh, 'Rwyn gweld o bell y dydd yn dod", "I see from afar the dawning of the day'.

The result of the poll was as we expected. Mr James Idwal Jones was elected with a good majority. There was a very able and attractive young man, by the name of Elystan Morgan, contesting this seat on behalf of the Welsh Nationalists without any real hope of success. I had a great deal of sympathy for this young man who was fighting and knowing that he was going to be badly beaten. I wanted our Labour candidate to have a really good majority but at the same time down in the bottom of my heart I was a little anxious that Elystan Morgan would not lose his deposit. As the counting of the votes proceeded, the bundles stacked in batches of one thousand for each of the candidates could be seen on a large table situated quite near to the Returning Officer. Before the announcement giving the number of votes recorded for each candidate I was approached by the man who was acting as Agent for the Welsh Nationalist. He asked if there was any way by which he could himself check the bundles of voting papers or could he ask for a re-count because he had some doubt concerning the bundles of voting papers on the table. He thought that some recorded for his candidate had been placed in the wrong bundle. I advised him that he could not check the votes but he had every right to ask the Returning Officer to do so and if he made such an application I would willingly support him. He went along to the Returning Officer and explained his fears and said that he had spoken to me and I had advised him of his rights. The Returning Officer immediately recounted the bundles of votes in our presence and it was found that a mistake had been made because there were 500 voting papers for Mr Elystan Morgan placed in the bundles for the Labour Candidate. These voting papers were then removed from the bundles belonging to our Labour candidate and placed with the papers for the Welsh Nationalist and I therefore in a small way enabled Mr Elystan Morgan to save his deposit. I never did like the policy of the Welsh Nationalists but at the same time I was always sorry when they were called upon to forfeit their deposit. In a later chapter I will again refer to Mr Elystan Morgan because there is a sequel to our meeting in Wrexham.

The By-Election at Swansea East

Continuing to deal with by-elections, I shall refer to just one other. It was in 1964, when we were confronted with a contest in Swansea East as a result of the death of Mr D. L. Mort who had held the seat for Labour since 1940. At our selection conference, there was keen competition and the unexpected happened in the selection of Mr Neil McBride who came down from Scotland after being nominated by the Amalgamated Engineering Union.

During the campaign, which was quite enjoyable, and, as can be imagined, during which we had nothing in common with the Tories, it was not difficult for us to get on with the Liberal Candidate and his Agent.

We were amazed when we saw in the town of Swansea a huge poster in favour of the Tory Candidate which read, "Take greater London pride with the Conservatives". This gave our supporters a great deal of fun early on in the campaign and this of course was good for our organisation. We pulled the Tory Agent's leg in a gentle way reminding him that the Tories now wanted to include Swansea within the local government area of London. In fairness, the Tory Agent said that the poster was a mistake and he could not understand how it had been sent down to Swansea. He took steps to have it removed and a more suitable one put in its place. I will leave the reader to imagine how the Tories were ridiculed on many of our platforms during the campaign. This of course was a safe Labour seat but there was great conflict between the Tories and our supporters and this had been so in Swansea for some time, which I think could be attributed in the main to our success in local government elections.

In between elections, I had for a number of years conducted weekend and day schools on the procedure for the running of elections including the points of law in relation to the nomination of the candidate. I had emphasised the need to be careful in the handing in of nomination forms to the Returning Officer along with the one hundred and fifty pounds deposit. The Representation of the Peoples Act mentioned the person who could hand in nomination forms, but the Election Agent was not included in the list though he could hand in the deposit. I was always conscious that a mistake could be made by one of our agents and

101

this would mean that the nomination would be declared void. A nomination form had to contain the name of a mover and also a seconder but also eight names of assenters, all having their names on the register of electors for the particular constituency. The last day for receipt of nominations arrived and we were invited to be at the Guildhall by 10.30 a.m. for the ceremony of handing in the forms prior to the latest time for receipt which was 12.00 noon. I should mention here that we usually took our forms in to be checked by a member of the Returning Officer's staff a few days before the closing date but the official handing in must be determined by the Returning Officer.

There were five candidates for this by-election — Labour, Tory, Liberal, Welsh Nationalist and Independent — and all were present with their agents and others. The Returning Officer, who was the Town Clerk, started to accept nomination forms for checking against the register of electors and the Tory Agent walked up and handed in all his nomination forms on behalf of the Tory Candidate. I observed what had happened and so did those who were with me on behalf of our Candidate. I was immediately approached and reminded of what I had emphasised in our weekend and day schools. I was told in no uncertain way that I should go to the Returning Officer and object on a point of law to the handing in of the nomination forms by the Tory Agent. I had no alternative, so I went up to the Returning Officer and asked him if the nomination forms on behalf of the Tory Candidate were handed in in accordance with what was laid down in the Representation of the People Act and I quoted the section. He paused, then looked up the section and called the Tory Candidate and Agent to step forward and he declared the nomination forms void because they had been handed in by the Agent. As can be imagined, this caused great consternation because they had in fact made a second mistake by handing in all their nomination papers instead of keeping one or two back in case of error. They now had to hurry along and have new forms completed and received by the Returning Officer in the very short time before noon. You can understand how difficult it was for the Tories to have a nomination form properly completed by a mover, a seconder and eight assenters with particulars from the Electoral Register. Well, they succeeded, and handed in a new nomination form just a minute or two prior to the appointed latest time. The Agent for the Liberal Candidate came up to me and said that he saw the funny side of what had happened and I confessed to him that I would not have objected if he had made the mistake on behalf of the Liberal Candidate. However, I was really glad when the appropriate form was handed in, even though there had been such confusion I really would not have wished to have a nomination declared void on what was a technical matter. Needless to say, we won the election with a good majority so we were able to relax again and prepare in readiness for any eventuality.

Festival of Labour

In the year 1962, there was a great deal of apathy in the ranks of the Labour Party membership throughout the whole country and that was understandable because the Tories had won the last three General Elections. It was, therefore,

102

necessary to take some action nationally in order to lift the morale of our supporters and, in particular, give new hope to our activists. The National Executive Committee, therefore, decided to have a Festival of Labour in London in which all sections of the Labour Party could participate.

Mr Merlyn Rees, who originally came from Cilfynydd in South Wales and was teaching in the northern part of England was appointed organiser. This meant him having leave of absence so that he could give his full time to this new, though temporary appointment. It is of note that following the Festival, Mr Merlyn Rees became a Member of Parliament and very soon became a member of the Cabinet, holding the offices of Secretary of State for Northern Ireland and later on was Home Secretary, two very important appointments.

I think the job as organiser of the Festival of Labour gave Merlyn Rees a great opportunity to get to know many branches of the Labour Party throughout the country because it was necessary for him to have their full co-operation in the task of co-ordinating their activities. He carried out his job with great enthusiasm and was meticulous in planning the festival, so that it was to be fully representative of the Labour Party in every part of the country.

The Welsh Council of Labour hired a six-wheeled float carrying scenery expertly designed by Mr Clifford Ashley. It, of course, had to be arranged and constructed in such a way as to stand the long journey to London and also to take its place in a procession through the streets of London.

On the float there was a girl in Welsh costume sitting in front of a spinning wheel, a coal miner and a Welsh dresser and suitable china. Then there was a huge map showing the Parliamentary constituencies with the representation prior to 1945 and the position in Wales since that date, showing that there are thirty six constituencies in Wales and out of that number there are twenty seven held by Labour members. As our float travelled through those parts of England on its way to London, it was given a tremendous reception and again the same thing happened on reaching London and taking its rightful place in the procession, emphasizing the part Wales had played, and was still playing, in the affairs of the Labour Party.

17

The General Election of 1964

We now move on to 1964 with a General Election which would give us an opportunity to fight very hard with the view to electing a Labour Government, because we had been in power for only seven years after our tremendous victory back in 1945 and now for the past twelve years we had had a Tory Government. We could not do much more in Wales because we had done remarkably well at every General Election but we went into every contest on the basis that every single vote counted. We in Wales held for the Labour Party twenty-seven of the Parliamentary seats out of a possible thirty six seats, so it will be seen that we held two more than we held after the 1945 General Election. As I have mentioned in an earlier chapter, we had no time in 1959 to adequately publicise that part of our policy in favour of the appointment of a Secretary of State for Wales. A policy making committee had been appointed to draw up our manifesto for Wales and this was in addition to the one for the rest of Britain. I was a member of this committee and had been on every policy making committee concerning Wales since 1945. We produced our document which was entitled *Signposts to a New Wales* which had the support of every Labour candidate throughout the Principality, I herewith quote some of its main features,

The appointment of a Secretary of State for Wales
Leasehold Reform as a matter of urgency
A New Town to act as a focal point for economic and social development throughout Mid Wales
A Water Board for Wales
To review the position of the Council for Wales

This new policy statement was necessary but it did not appear to have made much difference in our voting strength for our total vote was almost 4,000 less than we polled in 1959, but we did win Swansea West and finished up with twenty eight Labour Members of Parliament. When all the results were declared for the whole of Britain it was revealed that the Labour Party had won the General Election but with a majority of six seats only. It is interesting to note that Wales had again played its part and our organisation had proved its value. It was now for the Members of Parliament to decide how to function with so slender a majority.

The Rt Hon James Griffiths was appointed as the first Secretary of State for Wales with a seat in the Cabinet, an honour richly deserved. This was my swan song as Labour Party Organiser for Wales and in fact I should have retired in September 1963, but the National Executive Committee of the Labour Party asked me to continue with my work until after the General Election. I handed over the reins on the 28th of February, 1965. The Council of Labour presented me with a substantial cheque and a gold wrist watch, my staff in the office gave me the bracelet, the Council of Labour also presented my wife with some jewellery. The Carmarthen constituency brought to the presentation conference a small inscribed 'Coracle' as a reminder of the by-election in 1957, this along with all other presents gave me much pleasure. I knew it would be difficult to go into retirement but I thought it would be possible for me to sit back and perhaps do those things which I particularly wanted to do. On congratulating Mr Emrys Jones, my successor, whom I had known since 1945, I wished him all the best and made it clear that I would not visit the office unless I was invited to do so and would only offer any advice when asked to do so.

Retirement? Not Likely!

It was not easy to settle down and accept retirement as an actual fact particularly when politics had taken up so much of my life for I had been in the movement since I was fifteen years of age and therefore my active association goes back over the past fifty years. However, before I was given a chance to think this matter out for myself we were faced with the 1966 General Election and the National Executive Committee of the Labour Party asked me to take charge of the election for our candidate in the Cardiganshire Constituency, which had long been considered a stronghold of Liberalism where the Member of Parliament was Mr Roderick Bowen, I had, for years, held the view that this constituency would be about the last to fall to the Labour Party. I had to consider very carefully the request made by the National Executive Committee because there were difficulties caused by geography. It was so far away from Cardiff and indeed very far away in mileage from the centre of the political struggle. Then again would I be fighting a losing battle in this area which was, and had been for a long time, steeped in Liberalism? Our candidate was a young man named Elystan Morgan who lived in Wrexham but had some association with Cardiganshire, where he had attended school and the University College. This young man had represented the Welsh Nationalist Party as their candidate in the Wrexham by-election in 1955. My acceptance to be responsible for this election for the Labour Candidate was not easy because of the many considerations and I must make it clear that my doubts had nothing to do with the candidate. I had to consider that Mr Roderick Bowen had been the Member of Parliament for the past twenty years and it would be difficult to remove him. However in this there was a challenge, and though I had officially retired, I had no desire to sit back when there was a definite challenge to be faced. It was this that became the deciding factor. Off I went to Cardiganshire and opened an office in Aberystwyth which is the largest and most populous town in the County.

I was immediately given great support throughout the county and in particular from the University College. During this campaign, it was the first time ever for any parts of the constituency to be canvassed for and on behalf of a Labour Candidate. I must in all fairness mention two people who gave me tremendous support and were untiring in their efforts. They are Dr J.R. Hinchliffe and his wife who were at that time students at the College and these two students remained in Aberystwyth during the vacation and gave all their time to our election campaign. They in fact took over the responsibility for organising a canvass of Aberystwyth and the compiling of records that were of great value on Polling Day.

Elystan Morgan was a first class candidate and I cannot speak too highly of his ability and his understanding of the ordinary people. Furthermore he was a great platform speaker and able to demolish his opponents in all public meetings but he did this, and all the things expected of him, with dignity and courtesy, and throughout the whole campaign he was ably supported by his wife Alwen.

The constituency of Cardiganshire consisted of the whole county made up of a few towns, many villages and hamlets with a large number of farms. It was, therefore, necessary for us to consider ways and means of reaching the electors who, in the main, would be unable to attend meetings because of the rural nature of the area. It was, therefore, decided that our approach should be made through the printed word, but then came the question, how to get it to the electors. There was a weekly newspaper printed in Aberystwyth which in one way or another went to almost every home in the county so we decided to take a full page for the week before Polling Day. This meant that this weekly newspaper went out on the Friday and the election would be on the Thursday of the following week. It must be appreciated that in the rural parts of the Principality, a weekly newspaper would not be read and finished within a couple of days. It would in fact be kept for at least a week and would be read over the weekend and for several more days. To advertise political matters in the local newspaper was quite new in this county and took our opponents by surprise. It was a great success, for here was the local newspaper carrying into almost every home a photograph of Elystan Morgan, Labour candidate, along with a message from Mr Harold Wilson, Prime Minister, inviting the electors to 'Vote Labour'. We were not short of visiting journalists during the campaign because of the interest engendered in this particular constituency which had always been a Liberal stronghold. We had from the Press the usual survey of marginal constituencies throughout Wales though there were not many, but it was concluded that Cardigan would be held by the Liberal candidate. One journalist in his report stated that Cliff Prothero, an experienced campaigner, was in charge of the election for the Labour candidate, but Liberalism was too strong to be overthrown. The journalist in question came to my office and questioned me on how the campaign was being conducted and asked me to give a forecast of the result and I told him that Labour would win by a majority of 500 votes. He did not believe me and indicated in his report that Cliff, with all his experience, was making a mistake. I was interested in what was happening in the grass roots of the electorate and continued to remain optimistic.

On the eve of Polling Day we had a great rally at the King's Hall Aberystwyth, where Elystan Morgan made a tremendous impression and inspired all our workers to go forward on the morrow determined to win the seat for Labour.

107

Polling Day arrived and it was a treat to see our people taking every possible step to get electors to the polling booths and for the first time ever for the Register of Electors along with canvass returns in Aberystwyth used to full advantage. The votes had always been counted the morning following Polling Day but on this occasion the Returning Officer decided to count the votes immediately following the closure of the polling booths. This took place at the Memorial Hall, Aberaron, where there was great excitement amid the ordinary activity of the checking and the counting of the ballot papers. On the completion of the count it appeared that we had won and one or two of our supporters came to me and said we had won, but I had been too long in politics and had seen so many counts, for me to get excited until the Returning Officer told the candidates and their agents the result of the voting and that was accepted by them. It was my job to endeavour to keep our supporters cool to await the final declaration even though they knew that we had secured the majority of the votes. Some of our supporters again came to me and said, "Why wait? We have won", but I persuaded them to say nothing and to do nothing until the result was made known. My advice was accepted and the candidates and their agents were called together by the Returning Officer who reported the figures following the count but Mr Roderick Bowen asked for a re-count for which he was entitled though I am afraid that one or two of our people did not see this to be necessary. The Returning Officer granted a re-count so every ballot paper was checked and re-checked in great detail and at the conclusion, the result was given to Mr Bowen and the other candidates and their agents and this was accepted by all concerned. Then came the time for the official declaration which was as follows:

Labour	11,302
Liberal	10,779
Tory	5,893
Plaid	2,468
Labour Majority	523

This victory gave me tremendous pleasure but the credit for such a wonderful vote must, of course, go to the men and women throughout the county who worked so hard in the interest of the Labour Movement and it was my pleasure to have been a member of such a team working in unity when the odds were very much against us. Elystan Morgan went to the House of Commons and was re-elected in the General Election of 1970 and soon became a Minister of the Crown in the Home Office where he did a splendid job.

I was again asked to take charge of the election in Cardiganshire for the 1970 and 1974 General Elections but had to decline because I felt the pressure would be too great for me at my age.

Unfortunately Elystan Morgan lost his seat in 1974 and is not now in Parliament but I sincerely hoped that he would be again elected in the near future because we are very much in need of Elystan and those like him to represent us in Parliament.

18

The Common Market

Following the 1966 General Election, I thought it would have been possible for me to sit back, particularly after such a fine win in Cardiganshire, but I suppose when all things were considered, and having led such an active life, I could see things wanting to be done and furthermore for me to sit back in an armchair would be most unsuitable. I, therefore, continued to take part in what was happening not only in Wales but throughout the whole world. In 1969 the Rt Hon George Brown came to Cardiff for the purpose of addressing a public meeting in support of our joining up with other countries in the European Common Market. The Labour Party had taken a decision during the late fifties in favour of this country entering negotiations with a view of obtaining acceptable terms for our entry. At a subsequent date, the Labour Party took a decision that the terms which had been negotiated were not satisfactory and better terms would be required. There were at that time prominent members of the Labour Party who declared that they would not be prepared to agree to our entry irrespective of the terms. They who opposed our entry were entitled to their views and were given every freedom to express them. However, I had been an internationalist all my political life and was very much in favour of coming to some agreement with other countries on such things as a Common Market. I therefore went on the platform with George Brown at the Cory Hall, Cardiff. George Brown, for whom I always had great respect, was constantly heckled and indeed a small number of people made up for their lack of numbers in the amount of noise they made. They tried their best to stop George Brown from giving his address, but George was quite accustomed to hecklers and he had an advantage because he had the use of a microphone so he went ahead and delivered his speech. My action in accompanying George on the platform was not very acceptable to some of the hecklers and they tried to prevent me getting into the meeting but I was determined to follow my convictions and that is just what I did.

In 1970 we had another Tory Government and they accepted the terms for our entry into the Common Market, and this led to many bitter arguments within the Labour Party between those who were against our entry and those who were in favour of entry. I continued my support for entry and argued that there would be an opportunity to improve the terms from inside but we could do nothing from the outside. I took part in an 'Any Questions' session in my home town of Penarth when I was asked for my views on our entering the Common Market. I replied by saying that all present knew of my politics but I was in favour when we had a Labour Government and I had not changed my mind because there was a change of Government.

Then in 1975 we were faced with a Referendum to decide whether we were to remain a member of the Common Market or to withdraw. Personally I was not in favour of a referendum because in my opinion this matter should be decided by the elected Members of Parliament and they should accept their responsibility. In the campaign leading up to the referendum I spent a few months giving my full time in assisting the organisation from an office in Cardiff from where we covered the whole of Wales. On the eve of Polling Day the Rt Hon Harold Wilson, Prime Minister, and the Rt Hon James Callaghan, Foreign Secretary, addressed a meeting in Sophia Gardens, Cardiff, in support of our remaining within the Common Market. This was a very rowdy meeting because a number of hecklers tried their best to prevent either of the speakers stating a case. The chair was taken by Rt Hon John Morris, Secretary of State for Wales. He was quite a new recruit to the idea of remaining within the Community, because during the election campaign in 1974, he had declared himself very much opposed to our remaining a member. He argued then that he was speaking as one who had been brought up in a farming community. At the end of the meeting, we went along to the Angel Hotel where Mr Harold Wilson took me on one side and asked for my considered opinion on the way the electors in Wales would vote on the morrow. I replied that I was convinced that the people in Wales would vote by almost two to one in favour of our remaining in the Common Market. I think he was a little surprised with my answer, knowing of all the propaganda which had been poured out against our joining up with countries like Germany and France and he immediately asked me to repeat my answer in the presence of Mr James Callaghan.

It is now interesting to look back at the result of the voting in Wales which was as follows:

For Remaining a Member	869,000
For Withdrawal	472,000
Majority	379,000

It will, therefore, be seen that my forecast given to Mr Wilson and Mr Callaghan was in line with the actual result.

19

Devolution

There has been a lot written and spoken concerning the activities of the Labour Party and their attitude towards devolution over the past thirty-five or forty years. During the 1945 General Election our three Labour candidates for the constituencies of Anglesey, Caernarfon and Caernarfon boroughs published a news sheet in which they made out their case for a Parliament for Wales. Furthermore they gave their news sheet the title of *Llais Llafur*, 'The Voice of Labour'. There was at that time a newspaper published in Ystalyfera under the title mentioned above, which gave much support to the Labour Party. So it was fairly obvious that some people took the news sheet published in North Wales to be the same one that was published in Ystalyfera, or in any case, in view of its title, it would have been published by the Labour Party. This was not so and in fact those who published *Llais Llafur* in Anglesey, Caernarfon and Caernarfon boroughs did so without the authority of the Labour Party nationally or of the Labour Party in Wales. In fact they did not submit a copy before or after it was printed. It was unfortunate that people became very confused because the contents of that particular news sheet and indeed its title were very misleading. The Welsh Nationalists exploited the position against the Labour Party and at subsequent elections made reference to *Llais Llafur* published in 1945. I wish to make it clear that the Labour Party in Wales has at no time passed a resolution in favour of a Parliament for Wales. It is just as well for all concerned to have the record straight and I shall try to give it without fear or favour.

In the early part of the Second World War, during 1940-41, the South Wales Regional Council of Labour passed a resolution calling for the appointment of a Secretary of State for Wales. The man who campaigned for such a move was the late Ewan Morgan who hailed from Cardiganshire and was a member of the Executive Committee of the South Wales Regional Council of Labour. Mr Morgan also wrote a number of letters to Mr Attlee who was then the Leader of the Labour Party which formed the opposition in the House of Commons.

In 1947 we had succeeded in extending the Council of Labour so that it embraced the whole of Wales so we then had a movement which could consult with all sections of the Party throughout the Principality and make pronouncements on behalf of Wales. In the book *James Griffiths and His Times,* are found these words, "Cliff Prothero, a former coal miner from Glynneath, rendered great service to the Party in Wales by transforming the Council of Labour for South Wales into the Welsh Council of Labour. I regard this as being an important contribution not only to the Labour Party but also to Welsh politics, especially at the time a Welsh Nationalist Party was beginning to emerge as a political force". I link this with 1948 simply because in that year the Council for Wales and Monmouthshire was set up by the Labour Government, as reported fully in an earlier chapter. Following the establishment of the said Council was when the Welsh Council of Labour decided, "that there was no good purpose in calling for the appointment of a Secretary of State for Wales", and not since then has any resolution been passed in favour of a Secretary of State for Wales.

In the 1950s we had propositions received at the Welsh Council of Labour's office in favour of a Parliament for Wales. It was supported by men like the late S.O. Davies MP, Tudor Watkins, MP, John Morris and the late Lady Megan Lloyd George and others, but the Annual Conference of the Welsh Council of Labour turned down these propositions and made it clear that the Labour Movement throughout Wales was not in favour of Home Rule.

Then in the early 1960s a pamphlet was produced by Gwilym Prys Davies advocating an elected Council for Wales. A sub-committee of the Welsh Council of Labour was appointed which included non-members of the Council who were considered to be experts on constitutional government. This Committee repeatedly came down against what was suggested in the pamphlet and it was made clear that this was not the kind of devolution required. I retired from the Secretaryship of the Welsh Council of Labour on 28th February 1965 and up to that time the decision had been not to accept any proposal in favour of an elected Council. I am informed that the Welsh Council of Labour came down in favour of an Elected Council in about May or June 1965. Between 1966 and 1969 the Welsh Nationalists had some successes for they won Carmarthen and came very near to winning Rhondda and Caerphilly. I cannot help thinking that there was some panic within the Labour ranks and particularly within the National Executive Committee of the Labour Party and this is why they recommended that there should be a Commission for the purpose of considering if any changes were necessary concerning Government in Wales.

This recommendation came immediately following the by-election in the Caerphilly constituency and at that time I was sitting on the side-lines and will, I hope, not be misunderstood when I say that I was in a position to take an objective view of what was happening. However, it is now obvious that the Labour Party in Wales is committed to the kind of devolution which includes an Elected Assembly; it is no longer referred to as an Elected Council. I would like to make my own position clear by emphasising that I am and have been for many years in favour of a form of devolution and this is confirmed in the following extract from *Tros Tresi*, by Huw T. Edwards in 1956:

The Welsh Council

It would appear that the Labour Government 1945-50 gave a good measure of consideration to the resolutions that reached the head office from local Labour Parties in Wales. Resolutions demanding the devolution of administrative authority, and, indeed, a large number of branches demanding something more than moving administrative functions from London to Cardiff. Perhaps no one in Wales has been accused more often of being anti-Welsh than Cliff Prothero, and that without the slightest justification. I disagreed with Cliff on almost every aspect of Labour Party policy, nevertheless, I know that he had a burning love of Wales, It is true that he does not accept many of the particular criteria by which we judge if one loves his country or not. Cliff is a servant of

112

the Labour Party and his job is not to formulate policy but rather to see that the policy of the Party is carried out. He has, of course, the right to try and lead and to advise the Welsh Council of Labour, and the Council with its elected representatives drawn from four or five different groups. It is not an easy task, on occasions, believe me, to lead or advise them. I believe that it is to him more than anyone else we owe the beginning of administrative devolution. He had the ready ear of Jim Griffiths and a great deal of assistance from Herbert Morrison. I do not think that I am unfair to Cliff if I say that he also owed an enduring debt to his wife Vi, a Welsh girl from North Pembrokeshire, who sees the Labour Party through Welsh eyes rather than seeing Wales through Labour Party eyes. I am bound to say something else about Cliff Prothero – if there be any one of my acquaintance that I would be prepared to swear that he would go to the stake rather than see our Welsh Sunday going the way of the Continental Sunday, that one would be Cliff.

However in 1969 the Labour Government set up the Kilbrandon Commission and when the Commission reported in 1973 the Labour Party came out in favour of accepting the report. This was in my opinion a huge mistake but it must be kept in mind that at that time there was a Tory Government. In 1974 there was another change of Government with the Labour Party winning the General Election. However the word 'devolution' was hardly mentioned during the campaign leading up to the election, but though we had officially made a promise and had it recorded in our Manifesto, it is worthy of note that the Labour Party in Wales lost three parliamentary seats to the Welsh Nationalists. During 1974 we also experienced the result of re-organisation of local government and though this was not completely to the satisfaction of the Labour Party it most certainly did away with need for an Elected Council or Assembly. Following the 1974 General Election, I wrote to Mr Harold Wilson, the then Prime Minister, and pointed out the dangers to our movement in the acceptance of the Kilbrandon Report. I made it clear that we had fallen over ourselves in an attempt to play up to a small number of people in Wales known as Welsh Nationalists. Mr Wilson with his usual courtesy not only replied but sent me a copy of the Kilbrandon Report and made an offer for arrangements to be made for me to meet Lord Crowther-Hunt, who was at that time holding a special appointment in relation to the matter under consideration, if I thought this would be of any help. Here I quote Mr. Wilson's letter — "No doubt Lord Crowther-Hunt, who I have appointed my special adviser on these matters, will be in Wales for discussions and if you wish to see him separately I shall be glad to arrange this for you". I wrote back to Mr Wilson thanking him for his offer and accepting same. However Lord Crowther-Hunt came to South Wales but did not get in touch with me.

I again wrote to Mr Wilson pointing out that the promised arrangements were not carried out. It is obvious that Mr Wilson got in touch with Lord Crowther-Hunt because the latter telephoned me from London and apologised for not getting in touch with me when he was in South Wales. He informed me that he had met the Policy Committee of the NEC that very day and their report was then sent to the printers, but he asked me if I would express my views over the telephone and he would consider if they should be included in the report of the Policy Committee. I was rather surprised that he should have made any such

113

suggestion and I informed him that I knew sufficient concerning decisions taken by a committee and submitted to the printers, that nothing could be added or taken away. I, therefore, declined to give my views on the Kilbrandon Report over the telephone.

In 1975 I wrote to Mr Callaghan and expressed my views concerning the proposed form of devolution to be given to Wales. He passed my letter on to Mr Edward Short, Deputy Leader of the House of Commons who was by now in charge of the arrangements to get the proposed legislation on devolution through the House of Commons. In my letter I had pointed out the dangers of the proposed Assembly which would after all be 'A Glorified County Council', and set up for the express purpose of giving satisfaction to the Welsh Nationalists. Furthermore I made it clear that I was not against devolution but there were different kinds and I did not equate devolution with the setting up of an Elected Council. Mr Short shook me when he wrote to justify his policy on devolution and here I quote from his letter, "I think it was in 1945 that the idea of an Elected Council was first put forward by the Labour Party in Wales". I replied in the following terms, "Unfortunately you appear to be badly advised on what has been happening in Wales. I am prepared if necessary to quote chapter and verse of what has taken place on the questions of devolution between 1937 and 1965. It is obvious that you and I are not going to agree on the subject matter of this correspondence and therefore no useful purpose would be served by taking this matter any further. I wish to thank you for taking the trouble to write to me". It was the end of our correspondence and I was not sorry, but was perturbed to find a leading Minister of the Labour Government apparently so badly advised and this I think is further evidence of what seems to me a panic experienced in high places. In February 1976 the Government published a document giving its views on the questions of an Assembly and asked the public to submit its comments, including objections, to the Welsh Office. I took advantage of the invitation and submitted a memorandum for which I received an acknowledgement.

The argument used in the Government publication dealt with two points:
1 An Assembly would do away with nominated bodies which are not responsible to anyone.

2 An Assembly would give a larger measure of democracy to the people of Wales.

Let me take these two points and give my views concerning them:
1 An Assembly would do away with nominated bodies. This is because it is contended that nominated bodies are responsible to no one. Surely this then is the fault of the Minister making the nomination for he is responsible for his appointments to nominated bodies. Does anyone really think that there will be no nominated bodies once an Assembly is set up? It has already been suggested by supporters of the Assembly that all the nominated bodies would be manned by members of the Assembly. From my own service on such nominated bodies in an unpaid capacity, I certainly found my membership

114

to be a worthwhile exercise in public relations.

2 An Assembly would lead to greater democracy. This is part of the argument put forward by some members of the Labour Party and they are most certainly entitled to their views. There are, however, other members of the Labour Party who argue that it is not necessary to elect an Assembly with all the expenditure which would be involved and the large number of civil servants working on behalf of the Assembly. It is true that the Assembly will be responsible for taking decisions as to how the block grant shall be used in Wales. This is now done by the Secretary of State for Wales and if any change is necessary this could be done by a very small number of people who would meet quarterly in Cardiff or in some other centre in Wales along with the Members of Parliament. An Assembly would certainly take away functions from Members of Parliament, for example in Health, Education, Housing and Industry. Discussions on these subjects would drive a wedge between Members of Parliament and the Electors.

We are reminded that the question of devolution was included in our Election Manifesto in 1974. This is true and it is difficult to argue against something which we have promised to the electors. However in our Election Manifesto back in 1964 we promised, a Water Board for Wales and the building of a New Town around Newtown in Mid-Wales. These promises were not carried out but they appear to be forgotten. There are those who argue in favour of an Assembly and in support of their case who have allowed their enthusiasm to take control of some of their statements and they misrepresent what the late Mr Jim Griffiths submitted to the Labour Party Annual Conference in 1943 and though they say he was advocating an Elected Assembly for Wales, he was in fact doing no such thing. In fact at the said conference, the late Mr Jim Griffiths was presenting a report on behalf of the National Executive Committee in favour of Regional Local Government with a two tier system throughout England and Wales. The report was accepted by a small majority but the Labour Government at that time did not implement the resolution because there were a couple of the big trade unions against it, and it must be made clear that it had nothing to do with what is now under consideration.

In a memorandum to the Welsh Office I summarised my views on the document issued by the Government as follows:
1 When the Labour Party in Wales decided in favour of an Elected Council it was to deal with local government matters.

2 An Elected Assembly is not required and would be too costly.

3 It would increase bureaucracy and cause divisions between elected Members of Parliament and the electors.

4 It would provide a platform not for constructive debate but for unfair criticism of Members of Parliament.

5 Local Government should again be reorganised in preference to an Assembly.

115

I went on to explain that the Labour Party appears to be taking the view that because a decision had been arrived at, no member is now permitted to express another point of view. Such a practice would raise the question of how it would ever be possible to change policy. Some years ago when there was a great argument within the Labour Party for and against a Parliament for Wales, the Party in Wales came down against a Parliament. The Movement however did not prevent members continuing their advocacy of a Parliament for Wales and records will show that some Members of Parliament did so at every opportunity. They were told that they could speak in favour of a Parliament whenever they wished, but it had to be understood that they were speaking for themselves and not for the Labour Party. Let me give another example. When the Labour Party in Wales called for the appointment of a Secretary of State for Wales, but later changed its policy, and came to the conclusion that such an appointment was not necessary, this did not prevent people making speeches in favour of such an appointment and not a word was said to prevent them. I found myself in a very invidious position because I am a loyal member of the Labour Party and more convinced than ever that the setting up of an Elected Assembly would be detrimental to the Labour Party in Wales. I expressed the hope that the people of Wales would reject this proposal when given an opportunity through a referendum and, what is perhaps more important, that there would be no recriminations within this great Labour Party but that we should go forward collectively to the fulfilment of our idealism which is Socialism.

The Referendum Campaign

The Labour Government after much pressure from Members of Parliament decided that the electors in Wales should be given an opportunity to express themselves in favour of or against an Elected Assembly. It must be said that back benchers forced a vote in Parliament and secured a decision that even though the result of the vote would be by way of advice to the Government, there must be at least forty per cent of the electors voting *for*. This was in reply to the propaganda that had been conducted claiming that the vast majority of the people of Wales were in favour of the Assembly. I personally considered it to be unfair to claim that such a high percentage should have to vote in favour in order to have their wishes accepted. However, the National Executive of the Labour Party and the Labour Government fell over themselves backwards in order to please the people who were advocating a 'yes' vote. The National Executive made substantial funds available for the Labour Party in Wales to secure a 'yes' vote even though they had been advised that the large majority of the people of Wales did not want an Elected Assembly. The Labour Government also decided that Polling Day should be on March 1st, which is of course St. David's Day the one day of the year when the people of Wales express their great love for their Country. This day was definitely in favour of those campaigning for a 'yes' vote and every attempt was made to link the referendum with love of country. I could not and still cannot understand how both the National Executive Committee and the Labour Government could have been so badly advised.

116

During the campaign we had several members of the National Executive Committee and a number of Cabinet Ministers addressing poorly attended meetings, calling upon the electors to vote 'yes'. Furthermore I could not understand why the Prime Minister should have been given the task of appearing on the public platform in Swansea without the support of any local Members of Parliament. This, surely, was a clear indication that a number of Labour Members of Parliament were not in support of the proposed Assembly. In fact, it was well known that the Welsh Labour Group in the House of Commons was split down the middle. I felt really sorry for our Prime Minister having to advocate a cause for which there was little support in the ranks of the Labour Movement. There was nothing that I could do about it because I had indicated to the leaders of the Parliamentary Labour Party that Labour Party voters would not support the Assembly.

The campaign brought together strange associations because those of us opposing the Assembly found we were taking the same line as the Tories. However, I linked up with a group of Labour members who were in opposition to the official Labour Party policy. I therefore, wrote to the Secretary of this particular group suggesting that not one of us should appear on any platform nor indeed take part along with any Tory in radio or television programmes. I am afraid that things did not work out in accordance with the wishes I had expressed. Those who were supporting the Assembly were in a more difficult position, because their ranks were made up of some Labour Members, some Welsh Nationalists, some Liberals and of course some Communists. In fact, it was a sorry sight to see the Deputy Leader of the Labour Party appearing on the same platform with Communists and Welsh Nationalists. They were also supported by the national daily newspaper of Wales and I often wonder what the late Nye Bevan would have said if he could have raised his head. This question can never be answered satisfactorily but those who during the campaign claimed that Nye Bevan would have been in support had better have second thoughts. Unfortunately the campaign became very personal and degenerated into a mud slinging match which brought no credit to either side.

The Result of the Referendum

The referendum was conducted on the 1st March and the result was known on the 3rd March when the ballot papers had been collected and counted for the eight counties in Wales. I give below the figures and it will be seen immediately that not one county gave any real support for the proposed Assemby.

117

COUNTY - those entitled to vote		Votes Cast	% Turnout	Yes (%)	No (%)	No Majority
GWYNEDD	165,318	103,834	65.40	37,363(34)	71,157(65)	33,784
POWYS	80,027	53,520	65.87	9,834(18)	43,502(82)	33,653
W. GLAM	273,260	159,084	58.22	28,653(19)	128,834(81)	99,171
S. GLAM	288,610	165,912	59,48	21,830(13)	144,186(84)	122,355
DYFED	245,071	180,359	85.43	44,849(28)	114,947(72)	70,088
CLWYD	282,273	145,780	51.62	31,384(22)	114,119(78)	82.735
M. GLAM	388,587	232,026	59.40	46,747(20)	184,186(80)	137,440
GWENT	316,931	176,947	55.83	21,389(12)	155,388(88)	134,020
WALES	2,038,049	1,203,422	59,04	243,048(20)	956,380(80)	713,282

The electors declared in no uncertain terms that they wanted nothing to do with an Assembly which was very costly and yet had no teeth. I do not wish to prolong the discussion other than to state that I had known for some time that the people of Wales did not favour the proposal and in fact this had been made known to our Leader and Deputy Leader of the Labour Party.

'Tis not too late to seek a newer world.'

Tennyson